Chartering Fundamentals

Text Editor --- Cindy Wise

Technical Review --- Peter Isler, Robert Johnstone, Martin Mc Carthy Harry Munns, Lenny Shabes

Photography --- Lenny Shabes

Photographic Models --- Drew Curran, Gretchen Garnett, Karen Hennessey, Cathy Kachurka, Peggy Bedard, Don Mattera

Illustrations/Layout --- Vince Mattera

Layout/Typography --- Laserworks/Marty Capsuto

Published by the American Sailing Association

Photographic Subject Yachts Provided by --- Catalina Yachts, Morgan Yachts

INTERNATIONAL MARINE PUBLISHING COMPANY

Published by the American Sailing Association
13922 Marquesas Way
Marina del Rey, CA 90292

ISBN: 0-87742-955-3

TABLE OF CONTENTS

SECTION I --- INTRODUCTION TO THE CHARTER YACHT

SECTION II --- SAILING THE CHARTER YACHT

SECTION III --- ENGINES AND MANEUVERING UNDER POWER

SECTION IV --- PASSAGE MAKING

SECTION V --- LIVING ABOARD AND LIFE AT ANCHOR

INDEX AND APPENDIX

SHIP'S LOG

Vessel: Adventurer II   **Captain:** Harry Munns   **Date:** August 6, 1986
Location: Chatham, MA   **Destination:** Nantucket   **Forecast:** Fair
Fuel: 60 Gal.   **Water:** 85 Gal.

Notes:

Dockside check list revealed the chartered Catalina 36 was surprisingly sea-worthy and well equipped. Provisioning, crew orientation and a quick check of local knowledge preceded our 1535 departure. Warm sunshine, azure skies and a brisk 15 knot beam wind triggered memories of bygone days cruising these very same waters. Glorious summer!

We managed to keep Handkerchief shoal to port and rounded Brant Point just as the orange ball of a sun dipped below the starboard rail. With anchor set and topsides secure for the night, we set about the delicate business of food, drink and visiting with friends old and new.

Date: August 7, 1986   **Location:** Nantucket   **Destination:** Falmouth/
Martha's Vineyard

Forecast: Fair   **Fuel:** 59 Gal.   **Water:** 75 Gal.

Notes:

0500 hours wake-up was not a part of this island paradise the crew yearned to experience. Yet, the breathless pastel tranquility and a chance to watch sea birds awaken and travel their morning route made us feel like privileged guests. The captain was forgiven for the moment.

Our daily check list complete, we motored out to the Sound and headed for the Tuckernuck Shoal buoy. A 10 knot breeze settled in on our starboard quarter as we rounded the mark. As it filled in, we thanked the appropriate powers for a swift, flat ride down the sound. All parties present had endured the gamut of other conditions and preferred these.

Adventurer II's early morning departure was made necessary by a pre-arranged appointment in Falmouth. As the 1100 hours meeting time came and went, the captain made a mental note never to plan to meet anyone anywhere while on charter. Otherwise, the crew's internal clock cannot remain on "island time" and who knows what consequences might follow.

History reveals that famous and obscure mariners alike log both failures and successes. And so the captain's temptation to end this log entry will be resisted until the entire story is told.

At approximately 1200 hours a three bearing fix placed us just outside Edgartown Harbor. By 1245 Adventurer II was set about a mile off course and headed into Vineyard Haven. The causes were simple, an unexpected 4 knot current (actually it was expected by everyone but the skipper and crew of Adventurer II who neglected to consult the tidal current tables) and using an experimental aid to navigation, the moving ferry. It should be noted that this experiment has succeeded in the past but only when the skipper chose ferries headed in the right direction.

Columbus set a precedent for sailors which has gone largely unheralded through the centuries. He tried to get to the East by going West. He never reached his destination, proving that every shortcut has its price.

INTRODUCTION

Chartering Fundamentals occupies a treasured place in chart tables, corporate headquarters, sea bags and lunch pails throughout the world. Wherever images of tropical beaches, palm trees and shoreside retreats dominate sailors' thoughts, the need for greater knowledge will surely follow. Before very long, new sailors discover that each daysail becomes an invitation to more distant sojourns. Each harbor, lake and beach spawns a curiosity about more distant and more exotic settings. Who would have believed that sailing lessons on the bay aboard a Capri 25 would lead to sunset at Virgin Gorda's Bitter End Yacht Club in the cockpit of a Morgan '41?

Every year thousands of dreamers, like you, sail to the Bitter End and many other exotic locations. In recent years, bareboat chartering has become a highly organized form of sailing vacation that even relatively inexperienced sailors can enjoy.

Dozens of reputable companies now compete for your business, in cruising areas as widely diverse as New Zealand, the Caribbean, and the Great Lakes. Charter companies will need to know if you have the specific skills needed to sail a larger vessel in open water, to live aboard, make passages to strange anchorages, and to navigate safely. What do you do if you run aground, spring a leak, or the dinghy bumps your stern at night? Each question corresponds to a specific answer and acquired skill. The ASA has developed this manual to teach you the basic skills, to provide certification that will be accepted, with suitable additional experience, by charter companies in major charter areas of the world.

Chartering Fundamentals is divided into five sections. The first describes the basic features of a typical charter yacht and some basic handling features under power. Section 2 takes you to sea, to get the feel of a larger sailing boat, to practice such maneuvers as "heaving-to" and recovering a "man overboard". The third lesson has you working the yacht under power, in open water and confined spaces. Sections 4 and 5 should be taken close together, or simultaneously, for they are built around a 48-hour passage to an anchorage some distance away. They cover passage-making and living aboard, as well as the dinghy that makes such a difference to the enjoyment of your charter.

When you have completed the five lessons, you can challenge the certification standard administered by an AMERICAN SAILING ASSOCIATION certified instructor. Chartering Fundamentals prepares ASA Basic Coastal Cruising sailors for their next step, Bareboat Charter certification. Charter Companies around the world now recognize and in some cases require, ASA certifications.

Chartering Fundamentals, alone, like any book, offers only a portion of the learning process. Professional guidance, experience and refinement will complete the process and turn the neophyte into a knowledgeable veteran. The boats, the palm trees and the balmy breezes are out there waiting. The only thing missing is you!

THE AMERICAN SAILING ASSOCIATION

The American Sailing Association is an association of sailors, sailing instructors, sailing schools and charter fleets. Our purpose is to bring organization and professional standards to the sailing industry.

The heart of the ASA program is a comprehensive set of sailing Standards, which are detailed in the ASA Cruising Log Book. These performance objectives allow sailors to be evaluated on their sailing knowledge and seamanship skills. But more importantly, through certification to these Standards, the ASA provides the individual with a way to prove these abilities to rental and charter fleets throughout the country and around the world.

Sailors obtain certification in two ways. Many individuals attend sailing schools whose courses lead to certification. Others visit an affiliated sailing school and "challenge" the Standard. By comparing their own knowledge and experience with the published Standards, thay are able to determine what Standard to challenge. Then they visit a sailing school for ashore knowledge and afloat skills testing.

With the ASA Logbook, the Standards, certification and record of sailing experience, the ASA sailor has a passport to present to charter and rental agents in any of the thousands of sailing areas to which he or she may travel. Instead of having to decipher two or three pages of a sailing resume, the charter company can be presented with an internationally recognized Logbook that documents both knowledge and experience.

The sailing student can determine ahead of time what skills will have to be learned and what level of performance is required at each of the 7 student Standards of certification.

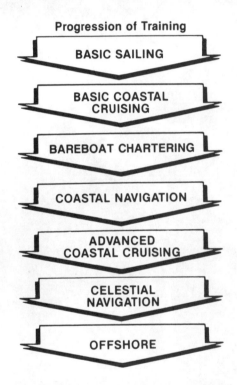

The American Sailing Association is a membership organization dedicated to boating safety through education. In addition to our schools, charter company and instructor members, individuals may participate in the ASA by joining as members. There is more on individual membership in the Appendix.

The American Sailing Association is dedicated to ensuring that every sailor learns to sail properly and is able to prove his or her ability to sail. The ASA's purpose is to serve sailors across the United States, no matter where they sail.

Course Overview and Objectives

The ASA Bareboat Chartering Course, which this book is designed to supplement, is divided into five sections. Although many of the subjects herein are introduced at their most basic level, the Course is a continuation of the **ASA Progression of Training**. Sailors certified to **Basic Sailing** (BSS) and **Basic Coastal Cruising** (BCC) may apply the knowledge in **Chartering Fundamentals** to their next certification level, **Bareboat Chartering**.

The Bareboat Chartering Standard is a more advanced cruising Standard for individuals with cruising experience. The individual can act as skipper on a 30-50 foot boat sailing by day in coastal waters. The Standard includes knowledge of boat systems, maintenance and more advanced sailing techniques.

Sailing and seamanship are skills, and like any other skill, expertise develops in stages. Therefore, <u>Chartering Fundamentals</u> deals with a specific set of subjects within the wide spectrum of sailing knowledge. This book expands on some familiar subjects from <u>Sailing Fundamentals</u> and introduces new ideas which will be more fully developed in other ASA texts.

Readers seeking definitive references for any individual subject should consult the Bibliography or card catalogue at their local library.

SECTION 1
INTRODUCTION TO THE CHARTER YACHT

ASHORE KNOWLEDGE

This book is divided into six sections, two parts each. The first part of each section deals with ASHORE KNOWLEDGE, usually general knowledge that you will later apply afloat. This ashore information includes basic terminology, some official regulations, and safety precautions.

The AFLOAT SKILLS part of each section follows the ashore knowledge. It describes the exercises and maneuvers on the water that introduce you to the skills needed to skipper a bareboat on your own. Each of these exercises is designed to teach a specific skill. They are cumulative in nature so that you progressively apply skills learned in earlier lessons and become ever more competent and versatile as a bareboat skipper.

Each AFLOAT SKILLS section has been designed as a one to three hour sailing lesson. On each occasion, the exercise is undertaken with a qualified instructor aboard. Bareboat charter cruises call on your skills under both power and sail. The course is set up in such a way that you learn the basic systems of a typical charter yacht, how to use them, and build on the expertise you have acquired to qualify for ASA's Basic Sailing Standard and Basic Coastal Cruising Certifications. Occasionally we will introduce a basic skill, then return to the same subject later in the text. For example, we will cover boat handling under power at a fundamental level in Section 1, then return to it in much more detail in Section 3. Think of this course as a cumulative exercise, leading to a certification that you have acquired the basic skill to charter on your own.

The course completed, the Epilogue tells you what to do next and introduces you to the exciting world of bareboating. We have, of course, included review questions at the end of each ASHORE KNOWLEDGE section. The answers appear in the Appendix at the end of the book.

A word on basic terminology. New terms will be accented in **bold** or CAPITAL LETTERS, followed by a brief definition (in brackets), if necessary. Illustrations or photographs are sometimes used to give a more detailed explanation of the term, if further definition is needed.

With the CHARTERING FUNDAMENTALS course students will probably be sailing a yacht over 30 feet long. Many of the basic seamanship skills are the same as aboard smaller boats. There are, however, constant differences due to the increased size of your vessel. The course assumes that you are learning in a 36 to 40-foot yacht, a typical size range in many charter fleets.

A point about seamanship as taught in this course. We give you general instruction on procedures to be followed when anchoring, say , or recovering a crew member who fell overboard. Our procedures are, of course, generalized, for local conditions vary all the time. A great deal of seamanship consists of judgement and common sense applied to local conditions, using basic principles that can be varied slightly according to circumstances at the time. We urge you to realize that this course is concerned with basic principles and procedures. Only experience on the water can give you the experience that distinguishes the expert from the novice.

With these preliminaries out of the way, let's get on with the first part of Section 1- a tour of a typical charter yacht. But before beginning our tour, we should define two commonly used terms:

Bareboating and Crewed Chartering

BAREBOATING is cruising under sail or power, where a sailor charters (rents) a yacht from a charter company or individual and assumes responsibility for skippering the boat him or herself.

Although many people go on crewed charters, this book is primarily concerned with the skills required to bareboat on your own. You can, of course, learn these skills by going on a series of supervised, crewed charters; but it is better to start with a formal course of instruction.

CREWED CHARTERING is cruising under power or sail; where the sailor charters a yacht complete with professional skipper and crew and assumes no responsibility for skippering the vessel.

The Charter Yacht

Chances are you learned to sail in a small boat, perhaps in an open dinghy or a day-sailor. Many beginning charter skippers began cruising in yachts between 20 and 30 feet in length. Whatever the size of the vessel you regularly sail, almost certainly she is much smaller than the average bareboat charter yacht in the Caribbean and elsewhere. Most, but by no means all, charter boats are between 35 and 50 feet long, with crewed yachts ranging even higher. This means that you have to learn to handle a much larger craft with much heavier displacements and powerful auxiliary engine.

Do not panic! The differences are largely ones of scale; sometimes involving heavier duty, often unfamiliar gear. Unlike the smaller yacht you are accustomed to, a charter boat is designed for living aboard for weeks on end. The skills you learn in this course are designed to help you make this transition.

The **Ashore Skills** part of **Section 1** introduces you to the equipment, systems, and layout of a charter yacht in the 40-foot range. It takes you on a comprehensive tour of the vessel as she lies at the slip. (There will, of course, be differences in equipment and layout from one yacht to another but these variations are easily identified and will be pointed out by the charter-company at briefing time).

General Feature

The basic terminology of larger yachts is exactly the same as that for smaller craft. Your BASIC SAILING and BASIC COASTAL CRUISING course defined such words as "hull," "cockpit," and "gooseneck," even if the hardware is somewhat different on the charter yacht in front of you. Take a moment to identify some familiar features such as the forestay and boom. Step aboard and sit down in the cockpit, so we can take a look round on deck.

Cockpit Layout

Although our illustration shows an aft-cockpit yacht, you can also charter a center cockpit design. Fashions come and go, with the center cockpit design especially popular in larger charter yachts. Experts claim the amidship design gives better visibility, a drier ride, and more space below deck for a separate aft cabin. In the end, it comes down to personal preference. Whatever the cockpit design, however, the basic layout will be much the same.

Sit down in the cockpit and identify the following features:

• WHEEL. Almost all charter yachts have wheels rather than tillers. They make handling both under power and sail much easier. The wheel is mounted on a PEDESTAL which

Figure 1-2 *The Catalina 34 is a good example of a modern fiberglass charter yacht with an aft cockpit. This design can accomodate a crew of six.*

Figure 1-3 *Charter Yacht cockpit.*

usually houses not only the steering cables, but the engine controls (see photo). The pedestal may also support a binnacle which contains the compass. Reach down the right or aft side of the pedestal and unlock the WHEEL BRAKE. Turn the wheel from lock to lock, noting the small piece of tape or lashing on the wheel spoke that shows you when the rudder is centered . (If the boat has no such mark, have someone turn the wheel while you look at the rudder from the dock. You can then mark the requisite spoke). Typically, two or three turns are required to move from lock to lock. Note that the wheel steers just like a car- you turn the wheel in the direction you want to go. This is in contrast to a tiller, which operates the opposite way.

• COMPASS. The compass is usually located on top of the pedestal, immediately forward of the wheel. Take off the plastic cover, or slide the shutter forward and look at the instrument. Identify the LUBBER LINE, the horizontal wire that is aligned with the yacht's bow. This is the reference point for steering your plotted course. Read off the COMPASS HEAD (heading) of the vessel in the slip, then close the cover. For night sailing, a COMPASS LIGHT is usually provided. The charter company will show you where the switch is located.

• COCKPIT SEATS AND LOCKERS. The cockpit is surrounded with bench seats, just like those on smaller boats. Usually, these are long enough to lie on at full length. Most charter companies provide cockpit cushions for the bench seats. They are rarely flotation devices and should not be treated as such. LOCKERS (storage compartments) usually lie under the seats, accessible through a hinged lid. These are

Figure 1-4 *Binnacle mounted compass. (1) Lubber line rests in front of the compass card number which indicates the yacht's heading.*

vital to you, for they provide stowage for important gear. Open the cockpit lockers and look for the following essentials:

• **Lifejackets** (personal flotation devices) **for every member of the crew**. These are required under Federal Regulations. Every crew member should know where they are located. If the charter company keeps them in another part of the boat, you may bring them to the cockpit.

This is where they will be used if ever they are needed.

• **Spare sheets** and dock lines.
• **Dock fenders,** used for protecting the boat's topsides against the dock. You keep these close at hand in the cockpit lockers underneath.
• **Miscellaneous gear**. This can include a LEAD AND LINE for taking soundings of water depth, buckets and scrub brushes, a stern barbecue, spare sheet blocks and winch handles, and the EMERGENCY TILLER. The charter company will show you how to install this if needed(see page 118).

Every yacht has a LAZARETTE, an aft locker located either astern of the cockpit or the aft cabin house, depending on the deck configuration. This is normally where the kedge (second anchor) and its line are stowed.

• HAND OPERATED BILGE PUMP. Close to the wheel is the waterproof socket for the Emergency Bilge Pump. Locate the handle in a nearby cockpit locker or down below. This is used to pump out the yacht in emergencies, when the other pumps may be inaccessible.

Figure 1-6 *Using a self-tailing winch. The serrated groove on top of the winch grips the sheet as you haul in on the line.*

• SELF-TAILING WINCHES. The smaller yacht or dinghy you are familiar with had jib sheet winches. The same winches on the charter yacht are much larger to accommodate much larger sail areas. They are self-tailing--that is to say, they grip the sheet as you crank it in.

• MAINSHEET, TRAVELER, AND SHEET WINCH. The mainsheet is heavy enough to require a sheet winch, a smaller self-tailer than that used for the genoa. The traveler is often mounted on either the main or aft cabin top.

• ENGINE CONTROL PANEL. Locate the small panel that holds the ignition switch, decompression lever if so equipped for stopping the diesel, and the fuel, oil pressure, and water temperature gauges. This is either inside a cockpit locker or near the helm (see photo).

This completes our cockpit tour. Let's now move to the foredeck.

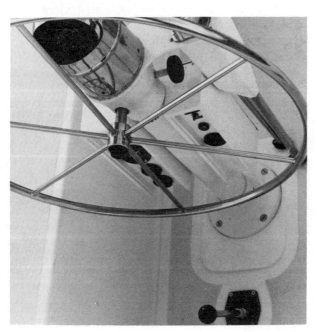

Figure 1-5 *Hand operated or emergency bilge pump.*

Foredeck

The FOREDECK, the deck area between mast and bow, is of vital importance on a charter yacht; for it is from here that you handle anchor and rode, as well as mooring lines. We start our tour at the bow with the:

• STEMHEAD FITTING. On most charter yachts, this is a complex fitting that acts as a securing point for the forestay, the roller furling gear, the jib foot, as well as an anchor line chock and roller.

• ANCHOR LINE AND ANCHOR WINCH form the remainder of the GROUND TACKLE (anchoring gear). Pull the 30 feet or so of chain out of the HAWSE PIPE (deck opening) or anchor locker. You will notice that this is shackled and wired to the anchor and line respectively. Always check this wiring before using the anchor on a charter yacht. Larger yachts like this always have an anchor winch which lies in the center of the foredeck. Most have electric winches, the greatest boon to the cruising sailor's back since time began. Locate the winch operating control, either a button on the windlass itself or on the deck nearby. If the winch is a manual one, the handle should be mounted in close proximity. Locate the CHAIN LOCKER either below deck or in a special deck well. Open this up and check that the bitter end of the anchor line is tied securely.

• BOW FAIRLEADS. (also called **anchor rollers**). These lie on either side of the bow, and are usually set into, or on, the CAPPING RAIL (edge). They are identical to those on smaller yachts, except that they are larger, with rounded edges to prevent chafe.

Figure 1-7 *Foredeck layout on a Morgan Classic 41, one of the most popular charter yachts of all time. (1) Stemhead fitting, (2) Anchor windlass, (3) Bow cleats.*

Rig

Now move aft to the foot of the main mast, so we can examine the rig. While the general layout is the same as on a smaller vessel, there are important differences.

Take off the forward end of the mainsail cover and uncover the gooseneck and mast winches. Two, sometimes three, halyard winches lie on either side of the mast. If the halyards are led aft, then they will be found on the cabin top by the main hatch; the halyards themselves may be of wire, with rope tails or simply all wire. Locate the halyard cleats, take each halyard off in turn, and trace its lead up the mast so you know where each one can be found in an instant. Also, look for the point where the other end is attached to the mast or rail so you know where to find them in a hurry.

TOPPING LIFTS (ropes used to take the weight of the main boom when the sail is stowed) are not found on yachts much smaller than 24 feet overall. If adjustable, the topping lift on our charter yacht is to be found close to the main halyard winch. Most charter yachts have a fixed topping lift that is adjusted by the charter company, so you never have to touch it.

Now remove the rest of the main cover and locate the REEFING GEAR. Locate the reefing gear winch (if equipped) and the stoppers or cleats for the leach lines if jiffy reefing is fitted; also the tack hooks at gooseneck. A few charter yachts have roller reefing gear; a company representative will demonstrate this for you. You may have to release some of the mainsail slides on the mast track. You turn this to one side to free the slides.

Figure 1-8 *Gooseneck area of a Morgan Classic 41, showing (1) Gooseneck and reefing tack hooks, (2) Halyard winches and cleats, (3) Jiffy reefing lines.*

Just as on the smaller yacht, the SPINNAKER POLE TRACK and its sliding ring lie on the forward side of the mast. The pole itself (often called the whisker pole) is stowed in chocks on the port or starboard side of the foredeck. Locate the SPIN-NAKER POLE TOPPING LIFT, which is usually cleated to the forward side of the mast, with the snap shackle stowed on the ring.

Many charter yachts have FLAG HALYARDS rigged from the spreaders to the lifelines. These are used to fly courtesy flags and burgees (see photo).

While at the mast, take a moment to check out the NAVIGATION LIGHTS. The PORT and STAR-BOARD lights, red for port, green for starboard, are on the bow pulpit or set into topsides. You will see a STEAMING LIGHT about half way up the forward side of the mast. The MASTHEAD LIGHT is often invisible from the deck, but is a valuable anchor light. Some large yachts have a pair of SPREADER LIGHTS used for illuminating the deck at night.

Jibs and Staysails

Most charter yachts are rigged very simply with a large mainsail and a moderate-size genoa jib. Some break down the sail area forward into two sails; a configuration that turns a **sloop** into a **cutter**, with two headsails. Cutters are quite common in charter fleets.

Sloop-rigged vessels are normally chartered with a ROLLER-FURLING JIB. With such a rig, the sail is set permanently by the charter company on a special rolling foil controlled by swivels and a drum at the base of the forestay. You can easily establish whether your yacht has a roller furler by looking for the rolled-up sail.

Roller-furling jibs are trimmed with jib sheets, just like their conventional cousins. However, they have some special features:

• FURLING DRUM. This is an aluminum drum at the base of the rolled-up sail. This rotates the jib during furling and setting by means of the:

• JIB CONTROL LINE. This leads from the drum back along the deck to the cockpit.

We discuss the handling of roller-furling jibs in section 2.

Only a few charter yachts ship out with a stay-sail. This is normally set on a self-tending boom (see photo).

Figure 1-9 *Base of roller furling headsail system. Jib Control Line has been completely unwound from drum indicating the sail is in its furled position.*

Safety Gear

Now check over the following on-deck safety equipment:

• LIFELINES. These run from the BOW PULPIT (stainless steel rails at the bow) to the STERN PULPIT and are designed to prevent someone falling overboard by accident. There are normally a couple of GATES in the lifeline about amidships, opened and closed with snaphooks. A folding swimming ladder either forms part of the stern pulpit or is lowered over the side from amidships.

• GRAB HANDLES on the cabin top are convenient handholds when moving fore and aft at sea.

• LIFE RING. This is often attached to the MAN OVERBOARD POLE with a safety line.

• FIRE EXTINGUISHER in the cockpit, usually in one of the lockers.

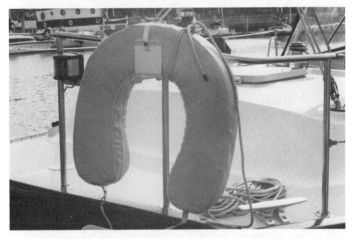

Figure 1-10 *Horseshoe life preserver (Type IV) mounted on stern pulpit.*

Figure 1-11 *Fire extinguisher mounted in cockpit locker near the helm. Indicator dial reveals extinguisher's condition.*

Below-decks Layout

It is difficult to generalize about charter yacht layouts, for interior designs vary from one boat to another. The accompanying plans show some alternative arrangements.

The layout below depends to some extent on whether you have a center or aft cockpit design. A center cockpit arrangement means that the main companion way leads into the galley-navigation area and the main salon. You reach the aft cabin either from another hatchway from the cockpit or in larger yachts, you can pass fore and aft through a narrow passageway between the two cabins that bypass the engine room.

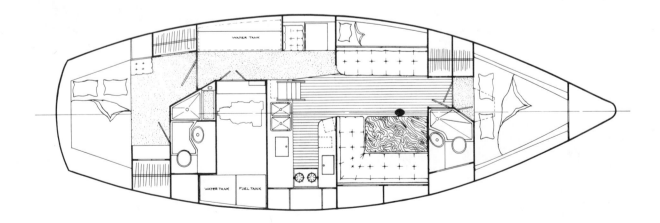

Figure 1-12 *Charter companies can usually provide diagrams of their yachts' layouts.*

Galley, Navigation Area, and Salon

The area at the foot of the main companionway is usually the nerve center of the ship, for this is where the main electric panels, battery switches, and other vital controls are found. Let us leave these until later and explore the Galley area first.

The Galley usually lies to port. Check out the three or four-burner propane or alcohol stove with oven, the lockers, drawers, and shelves for crockery and other cutlery, as well as stores and cooking utensils. The stowage arrangements vary from design to design and charter company to charter company, but going quickly through the lockers and drawers will give you an idea of what to expect on your own charter boat.

Open the refrigerator and locate the controls inside, as well as, the different compartments. Next, find the pressure water supply on the electrical panel and turn it on. Then operate the double sink faucets just like you would those at home. Open the locker door beneath the sink and identify the SEA COCKS (valves that let water in and out of the hull for specific purposes). We discuss their use later in the text.

Figure 1-14 *Sea cock for the double sink drain. (1) Gate valve turns 90 degrees between open and closed position.*

Figure 1-13 *A well designed galley features all of the necessary items within easy reach of one another.*

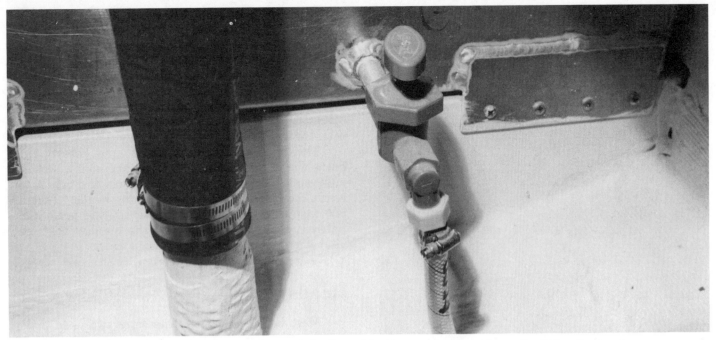

Figure 1-15 *Water tank valves control the flow of fresh water between the tanks. When both valves are open the level in both tanks will be the same.*

The fresh water for the galley (and the head sink, for that matter) comes from water tanks usually located under the salon bunks or in the bilge. If you look at the CABIN SOLE (cabin floor), you will notice some flush rings that enable you to open up sections of the floor or cabin sole. Pull them up and identify the following important items:

• WATER TANK VALVES. These control the flow of water from one tank to the other. Best leave them in the position set by the company.

• AUTOMATIC BILGE PUMP AND BILGE PUMP TRAPS. You should locate the trap for both the automatic main pump AND the emergency pump operated from the cockpit.

• ICE BOX DRAIN. A small pipe drains meltwater from the refrigerator into the bilge or to a hand operated pump in Galley sink. This is sometimes fitted with a shut-off valve. Should the pipe become blocked with ice box debris, you clear it with a length of strong wire.

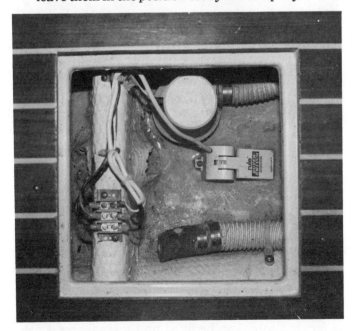

Figure 1-16a *An automatic bilge pump complete with float switch and screen filter.*

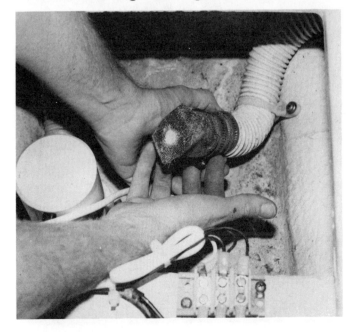

Figure 1-16b *Filter should be monitored regularly for blockage and cleaned when necessary.*

The NAVIGATION STATION may simply be the top of the refrigerator, in which case, you will have little more than a table top and a bookshelf to use. A sit-down table is vastly preferable. Locate the chart storage area, the navagation instruments, and the instructional manuals that are normally filed here. This is where you will probably sit when operating the VHF radio. Look for the call sign of the vessel near the radio.

The salon is the main social area aboard; the place where you eat meals when not in the cockpit and relax in the evenings. You pass through it to reach the fore-and aft-cabins and the heads. Take a few moments to seek out the ventilating ports and hatches, as well as, overhead grab handles that are vital when you are under way in open water.

Heads

Most larger charter yachts have two heads that are far more elaborate than the simple portable toilets found on smaller yachts. One is forward, accessible from the forward cabin. This enables two couples to have complete privacy. When you check them out, look for the shower controls, and especially the special bilge pump fitted to drain shower water from the head compartment. Again, open the lockers and locate the HEAD SEA COCKS, as well as, those for the sink. These may, in fact, lie outside the compartment, perhaps in the forecabin lockers or even the bilge.

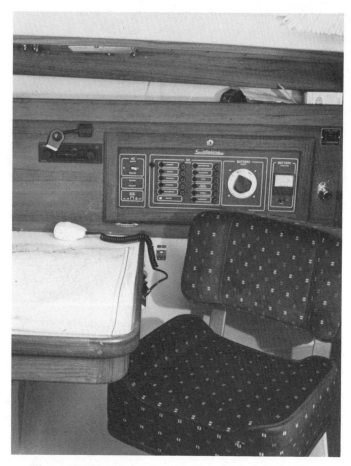

Figure 1-17 *Navigation station aboard a Catalina 36. The top of the chart table lifts for storage.*

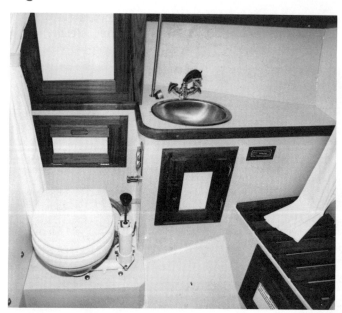

Figure 1-19 *Most heads will include wash basin and shower.*

In passing, we should note that the cabin sole in the forward cabin can be lifted up to reveal access not only to sea cocks, but to the through-hull fitting for the electronic log and depth meter.

Figure 1-18 *Main Salon aboard a Morgan Classic 41.*

Engine and Electrical Controls

All charter yachts you are likely to skipper depend on 12 volt power when away from dock. Lights, cooking stove controls, refrigeration, engine, anchor winches; all are battery powered. Most charter yachts have two duty batteries for this purpose. The electrical supply is controlled by the battery switch and Electrical Panel.

The BATTERY SWITCH is large and conspicuous, often colored red. It has four positions:

OFF is used when the boat is laid up or no one is aboard.

BOTH brings both batteries into use. You switch to this when starting engines, operating under power, and charging batteries.

"1" and "2" link up the power from one battery or the other separately. They should be used alternately. Keep the other in reserve while at anchor, in port, or sailing when the engine is NOT in use. This ensures that you always keep a fully charged battery in reserve.

Never switch between batteries while the engine is running. The power surge can cause electrical malfunction on some yachts.

The BATTERY TEST METER will be found near the main electrical panel. Use the convenient switch below the meter to check the state-of-charge of each battery.

Figure 1-20 *The battery switch regulates battery power to all systems aboard the charter yacht.*

Figure 1-21 *The switch below the Battery Test Meter checks the condition of each battery. In this case, Battery 1 has an adequate charge.*

ELECTRICAL SWITCHES on the MAIN ELECTRICAL PANEL control all 12-volt circuits aboard. Each has its own labelled switch including, sometimes, a special one for the engine ignition. Familiarize yourself with the most commonly used circuits like "**pressure water**," "**cabin lights**," "**depth meter**;" so that you can find them in a hurry - in the dark, if necessary.

Shore power circuits for such items as hot water and battery chargers are controlled by a separate panel nearby. These are only of use when the boat is in port with shore power cable attached.

ELECTRONIC INSTRUMENTS are controlled from the main panel, but the on-off switches are normally located on the instruments themselves.

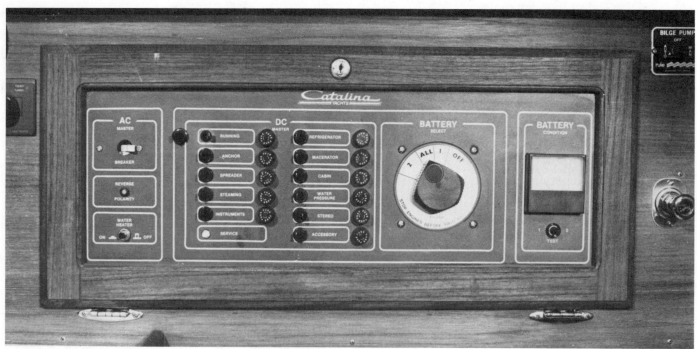

Figure 1-22 *Main electrical panel with labeled switches. Individual switches are turned off except when the circuit is in use to avoid battery drain.*

Figure 1-23 *Some charter yachts may offer sophisticated electronic navigating instruments.*

Legally Required Safety Equipment

Federal Regulations require the equipment that follows to be carried on all charter yachts in the 40-foot range. Locate each item, and check where it is stowed, so you can reach it in a hurry:

- **Personal Flotation Devices** (PFDs). The boat must carry at least one Coast Guard approved wearable personal flotation device per person aboard. Types I, II or III.

- **Throwable Personal Flotation Device Type IV** One of these must be aboard and immediately accessible in an emergency. All PFDs must be in serviceable condition.

- **Fire Extinguishers**. Coast Guard approved extinguishers are mandatory. Yachts between 26 and 40 feet overall must carry 2 "B-1" or one "B-2" type extinguishers, or one if they have a fixed extinguisher system in the engine compartment. Charter yachts between 40 and 65 feet long must carry three B-1s or equivalent (2 if they have a fixed system). You should consult official regulations for more details as to extinguisher requirements. In general, the more extinguishers the better.

- **Sound Producing Devices**. A yacht less than 39 feet 5 inches overall must carry "some means of making an efficient sound signal. Only vessels longer than this are required to carry a whistle and a bell, the former being audible for half a mile. In practice, most charter yachts ship out with a bell and a fog horn, either a freon powered horn or one that you blow".

- **Visual Distress Signaling Devices**. Charter yachts operating in coastal waters must carry such devices suitable for day and night use. They must be readily accessible and in serviceable condition and have not passed their expiration date. The charter company will have selected a group of devices that typically will include:
- 3 hand-held red flare distress signals,
- 3 pistol-projected parachute red flare distress signals,
- 3 hand-held rocket propelled parachute red flare distress signals,
- 3 distress signals for boats, red aerial pyrotechnic flares.

These are all day and night devices that can be used at any time. The charter company will show you how they have fulfilled this particular requirement.

Once you have checked out the mandated equipment, locate the following emergency items that should also be on board:

- First Aid Kit ,
- Yacht Registration Papers,
- Flashlights,
- Toolkit and Spares,
- Charter Company Instructional Manual, if any.

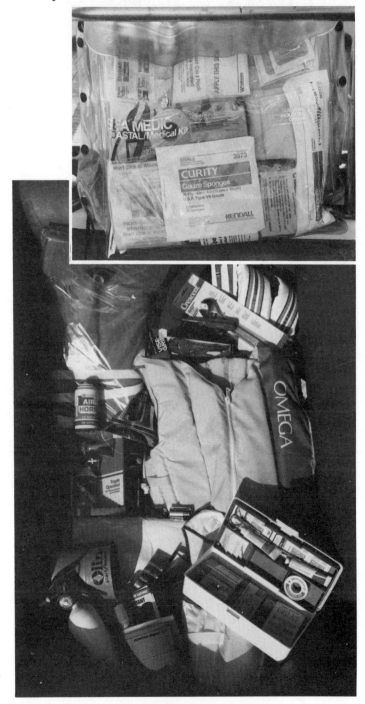

Figure 1-24 *Safety gear.*

Recognized Distress Signals

You may never need them, but you should know what the recognized distress signals for an emergency are:

- Red Star Shells,
- Continuous sounding of a fog horn,
- A gun fired at one-minute intervals,
- Displaying an orange flag with ball and square on it,
- SOS in Morse code,
- Mayday call on Channel 16, VHF,
- Parachute red flare,
- Dye marker of any color in the water,
- Code flags NC,
- Square flag and ball aloft,
- Waving arms,
- Radio telegraph alarm,
- Emergency Location Beacon signal, sometimes called a "position indicating radio beacon." These are not normally carried on the charter yachts.
- Smoke signals.

You may also make light or sound signals that cannot be mistaken for any signal authorized under the rules of the road or any recognized distress signal, " or "direct a searchlight in the direction of the danger, in such a way as not to harass any other vessel ".

We have now completed our tour of a typical charter yacht. She is basically the same as the smaller vessel you have sailed up until now. The only difference is that the gear is heavier, slightly more elaborate, and everything is much larger. Do not be intimidated! A few hours afloat will sort out the various systems into logical order.

It is time to go afloat, but first two more brief points about responsibility and safety.

DISTRESS SIGNALS
72 COLREGS

Figure 1-25 *Emergency distress signals.*

The Responsibilities of the Bareboat Skipper

The BAREBOAT SKIPPER is the person who assumes responsibility for the safety of the chartered yacht and her crew. He or she is the individual designated as such to the charter company. With a bareboat company, the skipper signs the charter agreement. His or her specific responsibilities are:

• To **organize the operation of the yacht** in such a way that all tasks are performed safely and efficiently. This includes delegating such tasks according to the abilities of individual crew members for different jobs and functions aboard.

• To **navigate the vessel** safely and responsibly with due regard to the safety of those aboard and those on other craft.

• To **operate the yacht according to the guidelines** and directions given by the charter company, including staying within cruising area limits imposed by them.

• To **maintain the vessel and its equipment** in the correct manner specified by the charter company. This includes carrying out daily and other less frequent equipment checks required by them.

• To **return the yacht at the end of the charter in good, clean working order** on or before the hand-over time specified in the charter agreement.

This course is designed to prepare you to assume these responsibilities, once you have acquired the basic experience afloat under supervision.

Figure 1-26

REVIEW QUESTIONS

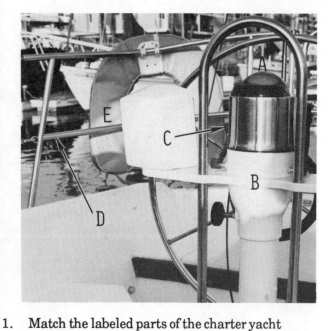

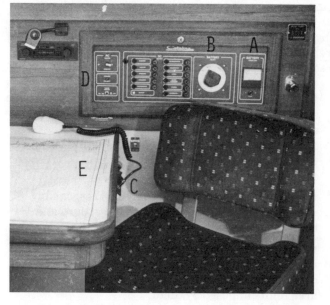

1. Match the labeled parts of the charter yacht identified in the accompanying photograph with the following:

    _____ BINNACLE

    _____ COMPASS

    _____ THROTTLE CONTROL

    _____ TYPE IV PFD

    _____ STERN PULPIT

2. Match the labeled parts of the charter yacht identified in the accompanying photograph with the following:

    _____ ELECTRICAL PANEL

    _____ BATTERY SWITCH

    _____ BATTERY TEST METER

    _____ VHF RADIO

    _____ CHART TABLE

3. List FOUR items of portable emergency gear that are aboard any charter yacht.

    a. _____

    b. _____

    c. _____

    d. _____

4. IDENTIFY the items of equipment in the accompanying illustrations:

    a. _____

    b. _____

    c. _____

    d. _____

AFLOAT SKILLS

Now it is time for your first familiarization trip. This is a short cruise under power, designed to give you the feel of a much larger yacht than you may be accustomed to. In Section 2 and 3, you will learn the basics of skippering a charter yacht under sail and power. However, before you set sail in open water, you should be able to take the boat out of the slip under engine power.

Delegation, Planning, and Judgement

During the course, your instructor will assume the responsibilities of "bareboat skipper," but will do so in such a way that the skipper under training gets to make the decisions - under supervision. Both in this course and in any "Cruise and Learn" charter, you will find that you are given progressively more freedom of action, as your experience accumulates.

Two qualities are important in a charter skipper and will be explained carefully by your instructor. The first is DELEGATION; the second, JUDGEMENT.

DELEGATION means that you assign specific duties to each crew member, not only steering during a passage, but every time you raise and lower sail, use the anchor, or cast off from a slip. This aspect of skippering is important because it means that every member of the crew is involved in operating the boat. It also ensures rotation of less attractive tasks like washing up, cooking, and cleaning heads or showers.

LIKE ANY GOOD MANAGER, THE GOOD SKIPPER DELEGATES FAIRLY AND CONSTANTLY.

Figure 1-27

How do you delegate? By matching crew members' skills with their tasks, being careful to explain exactly what you want done and how it is done, if necessary. If a crew member is anxious to learn how to hoist anchor, give him the chance to do it under the supervision of a more experienced hand. Then have him do it on his own. Be sure to rotate tasks on deck, unless you have crew who are content with the same tasks day after day. The golden rule of delegation is to match skill, experience, and the task at hand.

I always enjoy watching an experienced crew come to anchor, as I did once in the Virgins. The skipper was at the helm of the 44 footer, the crew ready with the anchor line on the foredeck with another hand at the stern bringing in the dinghy painter, so it did not catch on the propeller. The skipper passed through the anchorage slowly watching for sudden gusts and decided where to anchor, well clear of his neighbors. Then he made his final approach at just the right speed, so he had control right until the anchor went over the bow and as they laid out the line. Within minutes, the yacht was anchored in 25 feet and the crew enjoying a well earned drink in the cockpit. Not a raised voice, just a few quiet commands and nice judgement - that's what expert skippering is all about!.

PLANNING is as important as delegation. Every time you carry out a maneuver at sea, anchor, dock your vessel, or make a passage you should plan ahead. This course stresses planning very strongly, for experience has shown that the most trouble-free charters are those where the skipper has thought ahead, used simple check lists, and delegated responsibility carefully. Planning is merely a matter of common sense and logical thinking. There is nothing intimidating about it.

JUDGEMENT is the most advanced of bareboating skills; one learned only partially by formal training. It involves assessing weather forecasts, deciding when to reef, what time to leave on passage, whether to embark on an open water passage on a certain day, where to anchor, and a myriad of other decisions, large and small. This course stresses judgement as far as it can. In the final analysis, however, the only way to learn is through hard-won experience, based on sound training. Only the skipper on the spot can make the decision whether to use a certain anchorage or to leave port in the face of a potentially threatening weather forecast. Do not be intimidated by your lack of experience. Most decisions required on a bareboat charter are straight forward enough and a matter of common sense. Just remember that the ocean, or any large body of open water for that matter, is a harsh mistress, and that it will take advantage of any shoddy preparation or hasty judgement. Safety, common sense, and caution are the watchwords of expert skippers.

Checklist for Leaving the Slip

Use the following checklist to ensure the yacht is ready to leave the slip:

1. **Open hatches** and ventilate yacht. Check that there are no propane gas or HOLDING TANK fumes (onboard storage tank for chemically treated toilet wastes pumped out at special service locations. Holding tanks are an anti-pollution measure).
2. **Turn on engine compartment blower fans** to ventilate same if so equipped.
3. **Turn Battery Switch to BOTH.**
4. **Check bilges** and pump out with bilge pump.
5. **Ensure there is a PFD (Personal Flotation Device) aboard for each crew member.**
6. **Stow all loose gear** and personal effects in secure places below.
7. **Close and secure hatches** and opening ports.
8. **Explain the trip** to the crew and delegate tasks for casting off.
9. **Turn on electronic instruments** and VHF radio to father station.

Starting Engine

At this point, we will content ourselves with just starting the diesel auxiliary. We explore the major parts of the engine in Section 3. Here is a common check list for starting:

1. **Run engine compartment ventilators**, if you have not already.
2. **Check fuel gauge and battery conditions.**
3. **Check that engine decompression lever is pushed in and fuel supply is on** (this is rarely necessary on larger vessels).

Figure 1-28 *Pulling on the Decompression Lever will stop the engine. Be sure to push it back in before attempting to start engine.*

4. **Put engine gear lever in NEUTRAL.**
5. **Open throttle control** to starting position recommended by charter company.
6. **Switch ignition to PREHEAT** position and wait 15 to 20 seconds while glow plugs warm up.
7. **Turn key or press button** to start engine.
8. **Adjust throttle** to a comfortable warm-up speed (normally about 1,000 revs/minute).
9. **Check all gauges** for correct engine operation and that there is a flow of water from engine exhaust outlet located in transom or port or starboard sides. If anything is malfunctioning, STOP ENGINE AT ONCE.

Stopping the Engine

1. **Close throttle to idle.**
2. **Put gear lever in neutral position.**
3. **Pull out decompression lever**, or pull throttle further back than idle position.
4. When engine stops, **turn off ignition switch –** NOT BEFORE, as you can ruin the alternator.

Preparing to Cast Off

Another check list:

1. **Station crew on the dock** and aboard to handle lines and fenders.
2. **Look over the side for trailing lines** that might become tangled with propeller.
3. **Disconnect shore power** cable and stow away.
4. **Unlock steering wheel brake** and check that rudder is centered.
5. **Make a final check of engine gauges.**

Casting Off Under Power

You will achieve a smooth get-away if your sequence of orders is simple and logical. Before starting this maneuver, bear in mind that the wind will push the bow or stern faster than the rest of the boat.

Normally a yacht is secured in her slip by four lines, two at the bow, two at the stern. Sometimes, criss-crossed spring lines keep the vessel in place and prevent her from surging backwards against her fenders.

When moving in or out of a slip, remember that the rotation and pitch of the propeller affects the way a boat moves. It also affects the way she reverses. If the propeller turns to port in reverse, then the stern of the yacht will be pulled to port as she goes astern. You have to counteract this with the wheel.

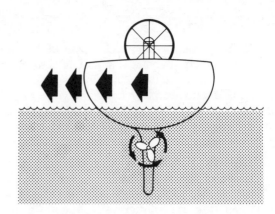

Figure 1-29 *A propellor which turns counter clockwise in reverse will cause the stern to pull toward the port side.*

Do not use full power astern unless there is an emergency. It places severe strain on the rudder, to the extent that the yacht can kick at you, out of control. Use moderate amounts of power whenever possible, except in short bursts.

Maneuvering out of a slip requires careful judgement, for you must have adequate steerage way astern to counteract wind or current setting across the entrance. If necessary, you should use a dock line to control the bow until the vessel is almost clear of the slip and the last crew member can come aboard with the line.

Once clear of the slip entrance, the skipper puts the gear lever in the forward position, applies throttle gently, and steers into open water while the crew stow away dock lines and fenders and stow them in the cockpit lockers.

Figure 1-30 *A little help goes a long way when maneuvering in tight quarters.*

Cruising Speed

Head for open water, well clear of the harbor entrance and shore obstructions . It is time for some basic exercises in boat handling under power. These may duplicate and amplify those in your beginning course, but are of vital importance; for larger yachts handle differently than small, outboard powered or auxiliary vessels.

CRUISING SPEED is the normal passage-making speed of the vessel under power with no sails set. Each yacht, each diesel engine design, has a different cruising speed, normally about 75 percent of maximum revolutions. Typically, this is about 2,000 revs/min. for a three or four cylinder diesel, as is normally installed in a 40-footer.

Once you are in open water, you should accelerate to cruising speed and familiarize yourself with the correct throttle setting. Practice setting cruising speed on the rev-counter on the Engine Control Panel, accelerating to maximum revs, then throttling back to cruising speed. Take the throttle down to idle; let it stay there for a few seconds. The boat will lose way. Then open the throttle until you reach cruising speed again.

After a few tries, you should be able to set the throttle at cruising speed very easily. <u>It is important you ask the charter company what cruising speed your yacht prefers. This will help minimize engine problems.</u>

Stopping under power

40-foot yachts are much heavier than smaller sailing vessels. As a result, they accelerate slower, turn in broader circles, and carry their way much further. For instance, it takes a 250,000 ton supertanker about 5 miles to stop with her engines fully reversed. You do not need 5 miles for a 40-footer, but you should learn the stopping power of your charter yacht. You must learn not only how far it takes the vessel to stop under its own way, but, also, with the aid of the engine at full reverse.

The stopping distance will be affected by both wind and current. If the wind or current are running in the opposite direction to your course, obviously the yacht will stop within a shorter distance. Alternatively, a wind or current from direct astern will cause the vessel to drift further. You may even have to keep some stern throttle on to maintain a stationary position.

Let us practice stopping ship:

1. In open water with no obstructions, **set the yacht on a straight course** at cruising speed and allow her to settle down. Locate a convenient landmark ashore that allows you to estimate stopping distance if possible.

2. With the helm amidship, **throttle down and put the engine in neutral**. Using a landmark ashore, hold the boat straight and allow her to lose steerage way and come to a complete stop. When she is stationary, estimate the distance she has traveled through the water while stopping.

Now carry out the exercises shown in the following drawings:
- Stopping distance with a head wind,
- Stopping distance with the wind astern,
- Holding the yacht stationary head to wind.

All these maneuvers are vital when anchoring or coming into a slip, and especially when operating in congested waters. Practice them until you are confident you have mastered the vessel's stopping power.

These exercises are an excellent way of understanding the differences between larger and smaller yachts.

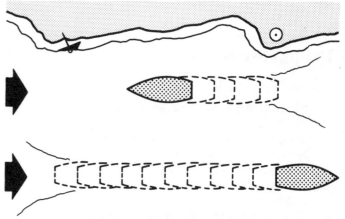

Figure 1-31a *Arrows at left indicate wind direction. Remember that a boat takes considerably longer to stop with a stern wind (bottom illustration) than it does with the wind coming over the bow (top illustration).*

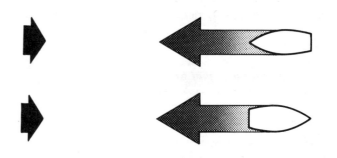

Figure 31b *In illustrations above A must motor forward to remain stationary while B uses reverse to neutralize the effects of the wind.*

Emergency Stop Under Power

You are entering a strange harbor with a narrow entrance in rainy weather. The entrance seems clear. You are yards away form the breakwater when three fishing boats come out at full speed, heading right across your bow. A collision seems inevitable unless you stop AT ONCE. This happened to me once off a small port in Spain. We went full astern at a moments notice and missed the second fishing boat with literally inches to spare. You must know how to stop your yacht in an emergency. Now is the moment to practice, when no one else is around:

1. **Throttle down** the idle immediately.
2. **Put engine in Neutral**, pause for 1/2 sec., then engage Reverse.
3. **Apply full throttle immediately.**
4. **Close down the throttle** as soon as the yacht stops.
5. **Put the engine in Neutral.** (This stops the propeller, essential if there is someone in the water).

Turning and Reversing

Now some steering practice. Find two or three covenient markers, like mooring buoys or racing marks that are not in use - or lay some fenders in the water on weighted tethering lines.

Now carry out the Figure-of-Eight exercise in the diagram a couple of times in each direction.

Next:

Steer clear of the markers, then turn the boat in a complete circle to port and then to starboard with the <u>wheel hard over.</u> This exercise will bring you back to where you started. Look astern and estimate the turning circle of the yacht. Now repeat the exercise at half throttle and notice how the turning circle is different.

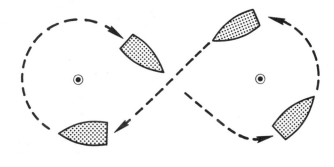

Figure 1-32 *Figure eight practice builds familiarity with a new boat's motoring and turning characteristics.*

Steering the Yacht in Reverse Under Power

Now find a patch of open water well clear of any obstructions so you can practice steering astern under power. Remember the forces that act on your propeller and avoid using full throttle.

1. **Stop the yacht** and bring the wheel amidships.
2. **Engage Reverse** with the engine idling.
3. **Open the throttle** about a third, until the vessel gains STERNWAY (steerage way astern).
   Once you are moving, the wheel will come alive, and you will be able to control direction astern. REMEMBER THE WHEEL IS REVERSED WHEN GOING ASTERN.
4. **Carry out the exercises** shown in the diagrams:

   - Turning vessel to port and starboard when going astern,
   - Steering a course astern using a fixed landmark.

The secret of steering astern is to maintain a steady, moderate throttle speed and to avoid major wheel movements.

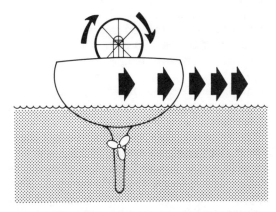

Figure 1-33a *Turning the wheel to starboard while moving in reverse causes the stern to move to starboard.*

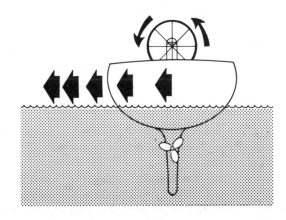

Figure 1-33b *With wheel to port, stern turns to port.*

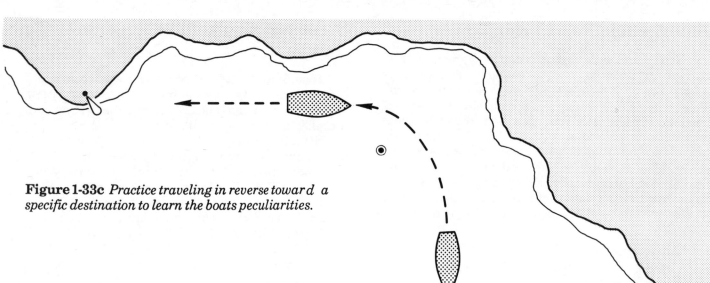

Figure 1-33c *Practice traveling in reverse toward a specific destination to learn the boats peculiarities.*

Turning Under Power in Restricted Quarters

Now you should return to port into an area where there are slips with fairways between them. We will use the basic principles you have learned to turn the yacht in her own length.

With the yacht stopped in a fairway where there is no room to make a 180 degree turn, you will turn the vessel in her own length using the wheel and throttle.

Again, remember the following principles:
- A yacht stops faster when heading into wind or current,
- The propeller pitch and rotation affect the way a boat stops and goes astern. If the propeller turns to port in forward, then the stern will be pulled to port, too, as the yacht reverses. The opposite effect will be felt with props that turn to starboard while moving the boat forward. You have to use the wheel to correct this.

Choose the spot where you are going to turn and bring your yacht to one side - the downwind side if a wind is blowing across the fairway. (If you are taking an ASA course, your instructor will set up the situation for you).

Now carry out the maneuver shown in the diagram, and practice it in different places several times. This exercise is like a three-point turn on a narrow road. In very tight quarters, you may have to make several trips forward and backward to get clear. This exercise is a wonderful way to master boat handling in close quarters, especially if there is a breeze blowing.

Once you have completed this exercise, you might want to practice backing into the fairway from the main channel several times and maintaining a straight course as you do so. Just make sure there are no other yachts using the fairway at the time!

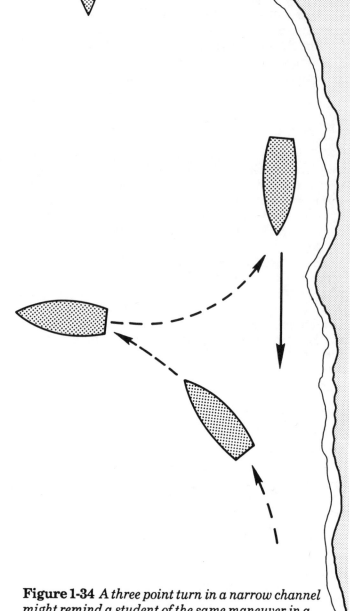

Figure 1-34 *A three point turn in a narrow channel might remind a student of the same maneuver in a car. Extra care should be taken not to roll up against the "curb", however.*

Entering a Slip Under Power

Time to return home! You have to use your newly acquired skills to secure the yacht alongside in her slip.

1. Well ahead of time, **prepare dock lines and fenders** and delegate dock responsibilities to the crew. Dock lines should be rigged on cleats and through fairleads with the coils looped over the guard rails. Secure fenders in their usual positions, but have one crew member on deck with a loose fender, ready to insert it between the topsides and the dock if something unexpected happens. Have the boat hook ready, the guard rail gates open.

2. Approach the dock and **observe wind and current directions**, judging how they will affect your approach. (With luck your first lesson will be in a slip facing upwind, so all you have to do is to keep the bow head-to-wind).

3. **Maintain a course at right angles** to the slips until you are about 1 1/2 slips away from the vacant berth, then begin your turn into the dock. Remember that a big boat pivots on her axis. Experience has shown that this is about the right average distance away to begin your turn.

4. As you turn into slip, **maintain the slowest possible steerage way**. Never stop, so you can make final alignment adjustments. This may require shifting between forward and neutral a few times.

5. As yacht draws alongside, **bow hand jumps ashore with the dock line** and walks the vessel along the dock. The stern hands now join him or her, as soon as possible, and take the stern line ashore.

6. **Skipper engages Reverse** and uses a burst of power to stop the yacht if necessary.

7. As the yacht stops, the **skipper engages Neutral**. Crew secures lines and checks fender positions.

Secure Ship

Our last check list of the day; one followed every time you use the yacht on a short journey sailing her:

1. **Stop engine, turn off ignition**.
2. **Turn off engine switches**, if any, at Electrical Panel.
3. **Battery Switch off.**
4. **Check that automatic bilge pump** is engaged.
5. **Turn off electronics**, if used.
6. **Centralize wheel and engage wheel brake.**
7. **Connect shore power** cable, if any.
8. **Check fenders and lines**, also tighten halyards to ensure they do not rattle against the mast.
9. **Close hatches**, take off personal gear, and lock up.

This completes Section 1 of your chartering course. All of the skills learned this time are a basis for later parts of this course. Next time, we will sail the yacht for the first time.

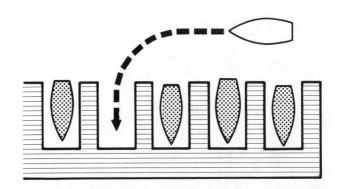

Figure 1-35 *Timing your turn into the slip depends on the characteristics of the yacht. Starting to turn about 1 1/2 slips before your berth usually works well.*

SECTION 2

SAILING THE CHARTER YACHT

Section I introduced you to a typical charter yacht in the 40-foot range. We took you through:

---

1. The basic layout and deck systems,
2. Below-decks systems and electrical panel,
3. Emergency gear aboard,
4. Responsibilities of the bareboat skipper.

AFLOAT WE:
5. Took the yacht out of the slip under power,
6. Learned about cruising speed and stopping the boat under normal and emergency circumstances,
7. Steered the vessel through various turns and maneuvered her in reverse,
8. Made three point turns in tight quarters,
9. Took the yacht into her slip and secured her.

ASHORE KNOWLEDGE

Section 2 builds on these fundamentals and takes you on a sail for the first time. The **Ashore** section is once again spent at the slip aboard the yacht. We show you how to prepare for a day-sail, and take you through the procedures for readying the sails for hoisting at sea. The Afloat lesson takes you out to open water, where we practice the basic sailing maneuvers that are essential to safe bareboat chartering.

As before, the course is cumulative. We assume that you have mastered the basic motoring procedures in **Section I,** so you can take the boat out safely into open water. You are the skipper as you cast off and power out into open water. Once the afloat part of the lesson begins, the instructor will take over as skipper, so you learn directly from him or her.

Getting the Boat Ready to Sail

We will assume that you have opened up the boat, and are now ready to prepare for a sail. Once again, the larger size of the yacht may be confusing. Just remember that it is a matter of scale. Everything is a little more elaborate and a little heavier. But the principles of sail handling and sailing itself are the same as on smaller craft.

Begin by checking every item of emergency equipment aboard. You may not do this before every passage on a charter, but you should certainly do so before setting off on the first day (see Section 1 for details).

REMEMBER THAT EVERY CREW MEMBER SHOULD KNOW WHERE THE PFDs ARE AS WELL AS ALL ITEMS OF EMERGENCY GEAR.

Now that you are satisfied the emergency gear is in good order, go back on deck to the base of the mainmast.

Preparing the Mainsail

1. **Remove the sail cover** which keeps rain and the ultraviolet rays of the sun off the dacron fabric. Undo the zipper or lashings at the mast, then roll the cover back to the aft end of the boom, releasing the catches or ties under the spar as you do so. Many people remove the cover from aft forward. It does not matter which way you do it.
    Many charter boats have a cloth of protective fabric forming the foot of the main. In this case, the sail is stowed on the boom by being rolled under the lowest, normally colored, cloth, then secured with ties or a continuous length of shock cord that hooks onto the other side of the boom. You can figure how to work this in a few seconds.
2. **Check the reefing lines** to see that they are rigged and that the sail battens (if any) are safely in their pockets on the leach. Examine the outhaul at the outer end of the boom. It should have been tensioned by the charter company. If not, remember to do so when you hoist the sail.

Figure 2-3 *The boom on some yachts rests in a Boom Gallows when the sail is lowered.*

Figure 2-2 *Topping lift runs from masthead to the end of the boom to support its weight.*

3. **Attach the main halyard shackle** to the headboard of the sail. Take the slack out of the halyard so it does not flop around. A good way of doing this is by looping the slack over the halyard winch drum (see picture). Coil the halyard loosely and loop it over the cleat.
4. Lastly, **check the gooseneck** and **mast slide track**, ensuring that all slides are on the track; the slide gate closed.
5. **Unfasten the mainsheet coil,** ready for letting go as the sail is hoisted. Also locate boom vang and cunningham, if so equipped.
6. **Check tension of topping lift** to see that it is carrying the weight of the boom. If the boom is resting in BOOM GALLOWS (a permanent rack designed to carry the weight of the boom when not in use), hoist the boom clear with the topping lift and tighten the mainsheet to prevent it slatting around.
    Now everything is ready for hoisting. Let's work on the jib.

Preparing the Headsail

Many charter yachts have roller-furling genoas, sails rolled on the forestay that are fully rigged with sheets when you arrive on the boat. For the moment, however, let us assume that the headsail (often called the jib) has to be hanked on and prepared for sea.

Decide on the size of headsail you need for the prevailing weather conditions. This decision is based not only on the weather forecast (see Page 75), but on the present wind strength, also sea and swell size outside the harbor. The amount of sail that can be carried in specific wind conditions varies greatly with the design of yacht. A CSY-44, for example, can set a large genoa in winds over 20 knots, a breeze that sets many lighter displacement vessels on their ears without a smaller jib. Ask the charter company for specific advice. As a rule of thumb, use the following guide lines:

- 0 to 15 knots. Largest genoa aboard.
- 15 to 25 knots. "120" genoa or medium-sized sail.
- 25 to 35 knots. Smallest jib, "110 or less", to storm jib.
- Over 35 knots. Sailors take up golf. Stay in port.

Once the headsail is selected bring the correct sail on deck and hank it on, rigging the sheets back to the cockpit, just like you do on a small yacht. Be sure to tie figure-of eight knots in the ends and to adjust the swivels on the sheet track, if any. The charter company will advise you about this adjustment. **Do not bend the jib halyard onto the sail,** as it may cause the sail to flap out of control.

Roller-furling jibs are already set and adjusted. You should never touch the halyard except in case of emergency. The sheets are already rigged, so all you need to do is to:

1. **Locate the JIB FURLING LINE.** This is run aft through special blocks attached to the gunwale or bases of guardrails. The after-most block is close to the cockpit. Find the cleat used to secure the line when it is not in use. The furling line also prevents the sail from unfurling accidentally.

2. **Check the jib sheets** are rigged properly, clear of life lines and other obstructions, and that there are figure eight knots in the ends. Glance at the bowlines in the clew. Sometimes they slowly work loose. You can save yourself a great deal of trouble by retying them now.

Figure 2-4

Staysail

Staysails are used on some charter yachts, especially larger vessels. They help reduce the size of the forward most headsail. This makes sail trimming and changing much easier for small crews. Skip the following remarks if the yacht you are sailing has no staysail.

The staysail is a useful sail because it can be used like an accelerator. It comes into its own on a reach. Set the staysail in a moderate breeze and the yacht accelerates like a train. In rough weather you can furl the genoa and go to windward under a reduced, all inboard rig that is comfortable in almost any normal weather.

Typically, the staysail will be stowed on its own SELF-TENDING BOOM (a boom set on a swivel on the foredeck). The staysail sheet is permanently rigged to the aft end of the boom, and is led to the cockpit. This arrangement enables the crew to trim the staysail for one tack. It will automatically assume the same trim on the other, while the jib is winched across and trimmed on the new tack.

Self-tending staysails are usually equipped with a protective lower cloth that acts as the sail cover, just like the mainsail. All you have to do to ready them is attach the staysail halyard, release the shockcord that holds the sail on the boom, and hoist. This is done at the last minute, when you are ready to hoist sail.

Some yachts set their staysails in hanks. In this case, you set the sail just like the genoa, except that the sheets lead to an inboard track, often on the cabin top.

Before leaving harbor, be sure to check the position of the staysail halyard on the mast, and to identify the winch and cleat.

Figure 2-5 *Self tending staysail.*

Other Shoreside Preparations

Before venturing into open water, you will almost certainly encounter commercial shipping, to say nothing of other yachts. A RADAR REFLECTOR is an essential in waters where shipping lanes are busy or thick weather can close in at short notice. These devices are designed to make the small, and often indistinguishable "blip" of a fiberglass yacht become magnified on a ship's radar screen.

A radar signal is like a light beam. It does not turn corners and "bounces" off your yacht, returning a signal to the transmitter. Unfortunately, the "clutter" produced by waves and the small size of your hull sometimes conspire to make the signal almost invisible on a ship's screen. This is where the radar reflector comes in. Most charter yachts have metal masts, but these only return a good signal when the spar is at right angles to the transmitter. As your ship moves around in the swell, the horizon's dip buries you in the waves. Even an expert radar operator may have trouble seeing you. A radar reflector is designed to bounce back a radar signal from a set of surfaces mounted at 90 degrees to one another, thereby enlarging the target on the receiving screen.

Take out the radar reflector from its locker and assemble the flat, aluminum plates into the familiar octahedral shape. Check that the angles of the plates are exactly at right angles. If the reflector is permanently mounted aloft, check that it is securely fastened. A masthead position is best of all, giving you maximum height, but some yachts have the reflector lashed to the backstay at least 10 feet from the deck.

If you have to hoist it, you should find a clip on the bottom end which goes on one of the wire stays as you hoist it on a flag halyard to the spreaders. A sail halyard may be preferable in extreme conditions.

Never sail in conditions of reduced visibility without a radar reflector.

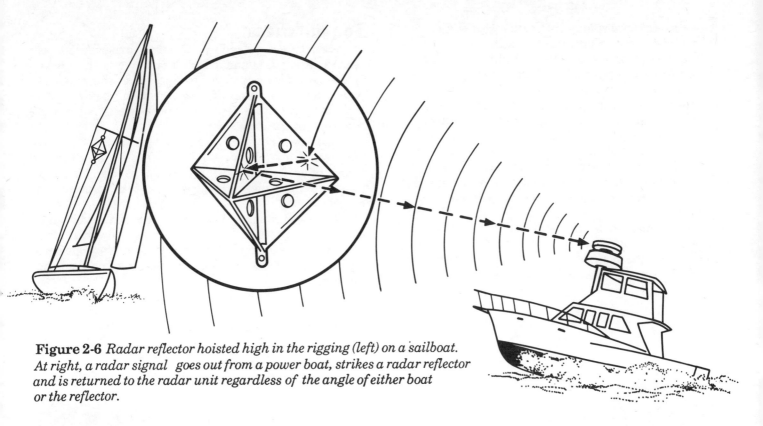

Figure 2-6 *Radar reflector hoisted high in the rigging (left) on a sailboat. At right, a radar signal goes out from a power boat, strikes a radar reflector and is returned to the radar unit regardless of the angle of either boat or the reflector.*

Sailing Clothing

The short session on the water in Section 1 and probably your fundamentals course have already made a few demands on your comfort afloat. A bareboat charter with its constant day passages and changing weather is another matter. This is a good moment before we go sailing to think about appropriate clothing for sailing comfort and safety.

The sailor's most dread enemies are wet and cold, for constant exposure to either not only reduces your enjoyment of the trip but adds to fatigue and can impair your judgement. The best way to keep warm is to dress in layers. Select fleece of polypropel for maximum insulation.

Whenever you sail in open water, and certainly on any coastal charter, you should bring along the following:

• A complete change of clothes, in case you fall overboard. Bring an additional pair of socks to be worn if your feet get cold.
• In cold climates, long underwear for night watches and cold days.
• For outer protection, thick woolen sweaters combined with a pile lined, nylon covered jacket ("Patagonia" is a well-known make). The old saying that you should take one more sweater than you need is so true. Take heed! A woolen hat and gloves are invaluable, for you lose heat through your head and extremities very quickly.
• Properly designed boat shoes which can also be used for extended walking ashore.

• Foul weather gear. Anyone planning to charter more than once should acquire durable, medium weight gear that can be used in tropical and temperate climates. Best purchase a two piece set with high-waist pants and a hooded jacket. Some designs have built in flotation and safety harnesses, but they tend to be more expensive. A piece of old towel around the neck helps keep out spray.

Figure 2-7 *A well outfitted charterer.*

- In areas with changeable, cooler weather a pair of waterproof boots and an individual safety harness are advisable. Lirakis harnesses are especially well-designed.
- A stainless steel sheath or pocket knife with shackle opener and spike attached to a lanyard worn round your waist. <u>Never</u> wear the lanyard round your neck. You could catch it on an obstruction and choke.
- In tropical climates a good sun hat with neck protection and chin strap. Sunglasses and sunscreen lotion are essential anywhere on the water.

The proper clothing and personal equipment make all the difference to your comfort and safety afloat. Take the trouble to equip yourself right from the very beginning. You will never regret it.

Figure 2-8 *A safety harness is vital for night sailing and night rough weather. The harness should be attached to a tether line and a light is helpful. A good harness will tow you by the chest, if you fall overboard, leaving the head above water.*

Sea Sickness

Nearly every sailor, however experienced, is seasick at some moment in his or her career. Lucky is the person who is never sick, even on the roughest days, despite diesel fumes, motion below, and cooking. They are few and far between, and even they feel queasy sometimes.

Seasickness goes with being afloat for any length of time. However, in these days of effective prescription remedies, there is no excuse for most people to feel bad, <u>provided</u> they take precautions ahead of time.

A few unlucky folk are sick whatever precautions they take. Even the most powerful prescriptions seem to be ineffective. Best they give up any notions of bareboating, for nothing can be done for them.

Fortunately, most people respond well to medications.

- **Try a non-prescription remedy,** like Dramamine, Marezine, and other pills sold over-the-counter in most drug stores. Taken ahead of time and on the time table suggested, they are effective for many mild sufferers. Try them first.. If they do not work:
- **Consult your physician** and ask for a prescription medication. There are various possibilities, the most used and usually effective, being Scopolomine.

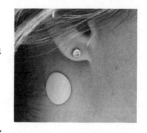

This comes in patch form. You stick the patch behind your ear and the drug permeates into your system for a period of about four days. Patches seem to be effective with most people, but are quite expensive. DO NOT TAKE PRESCRIPTION DRUGS LIKE THIS WITHOUT SEEING A PHYSICIAN, and monitor yourself carefully for side effects like drowsiness.

You can minimize the chances of sea sickness by avoiding heavy meals and greasy foods, as well as alcohol for about 12 hours before setting off. Get plenty of sleep the night before.

If you do get sick, try drinking water or eating dry crackers to settle your stomach. Hot soup or bouillon cubes can work wonders. Stay in the open air and try facing the wind, keeping your eyes on the horizon or a landmark ashore.

More severe cases should turn in and loosen their clothing, drink plenty of fluids, and get as much rest as possible. Victims should remain on deck and focus on distant fixed objects if some are in sight.

Some people respond well if given a job to do, like steering or operating jib sheets. Work can be an excellent antidote for mild cases.

A good rule when chartering is to make a safe anchorage as soon as possible if the crew gets sick. After all, you are sailing for fun...

VHF Radio Procedure

Before sailing, too, you should be familiar with basic VHF radio procedure. At this point, go below and sit at the navigation station where the radio is located. Identify the following radio controls and features:

On-Off switch.

Channel Display. This is usually a numerical display that indicates which channel you are using.

Channel tuning switch. This changes channels, each click denoting new channel.

Squelch control. You use this to reduce background noise. With the radio turned on to Channel 16 (see below), turn the squelch knob to reduce the hissing noise in the background. The proper setting is found by turning the knob to the left until the hissing is detected, then turning it back to the right until the hiss disappears.

Volume control.

Microphone and transmitter switch. This is usually kept close to the radio on a special bracket attached to the radio or nearby. A red or orange transmitter light on the set glows when you press the transmitter switch on the microphone.

25 watt switch for changing power.

Now you should look for the Call Numbers for the yacht, which are usually posted close to the radio. This three letter combination, let us say "WAR 2345" (broadcast as "Whisky Alpha Romeo 2 3 4 5," using internationally agreed upon code words), is the call sign for this particular vessel. You use it whenever you make a radio call.

Next, we should make a practice call. Try and arrange with another yacht to contact them at an agreed time on a specific channel. Here is the procedure:

1. **Turn on the radio** and turn to agreed channel. Adjust squelch control and volume.
2. **Pick up microphone and press transmitter button.** Check that the transmitter light is on. Speak clearly into the microphone: "(Name of yacht being called), (Name of yacht being called), this is the yacht (name of your vessel), Whisky Alpha Romeo Quebec 2 3 4 5 come in please, OVER." Release button.

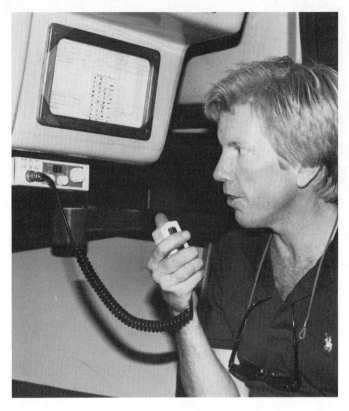

Figure 2-11

3. **The other yacht replies:** "(Name of your yacht), (Name of your yacht), this is the (Name of their vessel), their call number, loud and clear..."
4. At this point you will **respond, again using your name and call number** and either tell them to change to a specific channel, or, in this case since you have already agreed on one, transmit your message.
   Your message ended, you close with the word "Over." This indicates that you have completed your transmission, and await a reply.
5. **The other party acknowledges the message** with their name and call number. If there is no reply, they will say "Message understood, standing by on Channel 16. Out." This indicates they are now monitoring Channel 16, the emergency channel, as they would do when under way.

Figure 2-10 *The control panel of a VHF radio.*

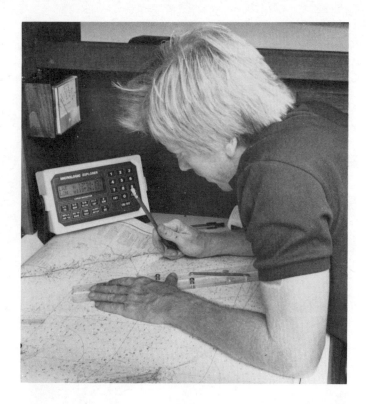

Man Overboard Procedures

The essence of safe chartering is to be prepared for unexpected turns of events every moment. Being prepared means having the right equipment aboard, and being mentally prepared for sudden emergencies as well. Of all these emergencies, none is more important than recovering a crew member who has fallen overboard.

Later in this Section, we practice two methods of returning to a crew member in the water in moderate winds. At this point, we describe two procedures for getting someone in the water back on board. This is something that is best demonstrated at the dock.

In your Sailing Fundamentals course, you learned that you should approach a person in the water to windward and get a line to them as soon as possible so they are secured to the vessel. How, then, do you recover them safely aboard if they are unable to assist themselves?

> ONE VITAL RULE: ALWAYS STOP THE ENGINE TO AVOID CATCHING THE SWIMMER WITH THE PROPELLER

Using a Line

One method of lifting a swimmer would be to attach an end of the boom vang to the aft end of the boom. With a large bowline atttached to the free end of the vang, swing the boom out and ease the vang. The swimmer places the bowline around his torso. The crew then hauls in the vang and swings the boom back over the deck.

6. **You end the interchange with**:
   "Name of yacht, call number, standing by on 16. Out."
   The word "Out" signals that you are finished.
7. At this point, you either switch to Channel 16, or switch off the set, returning the microphone to its bracket.

The charter company will tell you what channels are normally employed in your charter area. Normally, they will advise you to monitor Channel 16. This is the emergency channel, and is the one monitored by most vessels at sea. However, it is only used to receive and send EMERGENCY messages, or to establish contact intended to continue on another channel.

Most Caribbean and South Pacific charter companies operate regular radio schedules, where they contact yachts with messages, pass on weather reports, and so on. They will tell you which channel to monitor and at what hours each day. Some companies require that you report your position to them each evening, but this is usually only in remoter charter areas.

In US waters, weather forecasts can be obtained from the weather channels on your VHF. These are labelled W1 and W2 on the dial, or have a special control switch. These receive recorded weather messages that are changed periodically. They also broadcast hurricane, storm, and gale warnings, as well as tornado watches. You will use these channels to obtain weather forecasts before leaving port.

Figure 2-13 *Recovering a victim using the boat's gear.*

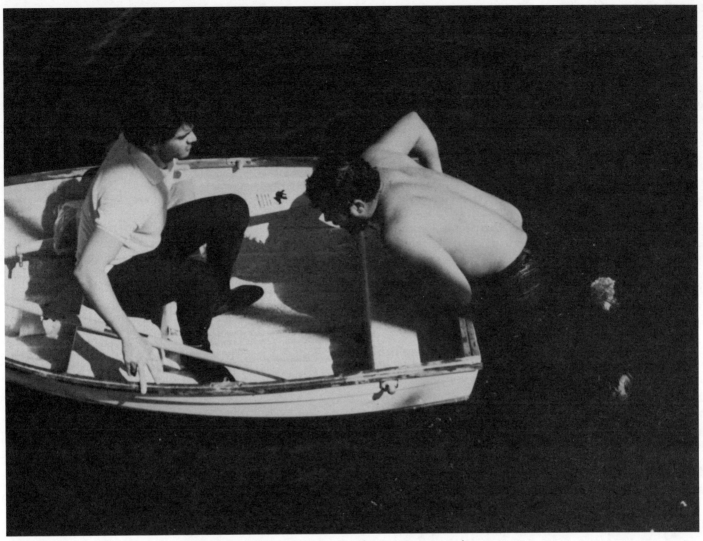

Figure 2-14 *Using the dinghy to recover a swimmer.*

Using the Dinghy

You can use the dinghy if you are towing one astern.
1. Have the swimmer hold onto the stern of the dinghy.
2. Bring the dinghy alongside and send one or two crew members into her.
3. With one crew member in the bow as counter-balance, help the victim into the dinghy.
4. If this does not work, bring the tender alongside, secure the main halyard bowline around the swimmer's torso.

If your dinghy is an inflatable, keep her half-inflated on the cabin top. Lower her into the water, so the swimmer can be pulled into her.

These exercises are fun to practice at anchor in a tropical bay. Best try them when the water is calm, before you need them on a day when the spray is flying.

Figure 2-12 *Boarding ladders can be used to recover swimmers in calm water.*

Sailing Emergencies - Crew Member Overboard!

Every charter skipper worth his salt mentally prepares for the moment when the dreaded cry "man overboard" rings across the deck. It is now time for you to practice the drills for recovering a swimming crew member without advance notice.

An essential part of the exercise is advance preparation. Every member of the crew should know where the emergency gear is kept and should know how to use it. We assume here that everyone does.

Your Sailing Fundamentals course taught you how to sail up to someone in the water, and we discussed three ways of bringing someone aboard earlier in this lesson. Your basic course told you what to do when someone goes overboard. Just as in a smaller boat you immediately:

1. **Shout MAN OVERBOARD**
2. **Throw over a PFD or life-ring**, as close to the victim as possible
3. **Make sure that someone is assigned to keep the swimmer in sight at all times.**

Maneuvering to pick up the person in the water is identical to the procedure in the smaller vessel, except that:

You have the use of a diesel auxiliary if you need it. However, there are new Golden Rules:

NEVER TRAIL LINES OVER THE SIDE WHEN RUNNING THE ENGINE. They can get caught in the propeller.

DO NOT RUN THE ENGINE WHEN ALONG - SIDE SOMEONE IN THE WATER...

DO NOT START THE ENGINE IN CASE THE PROPELLER CATCHES THE VICTIM.

In fact, it is best not to use the engine when recovering a person overboard if you can possibly avoid it.

During this lesson, you will practice picking up an object under sail, using the procedures taught in your basic course. The instructor may surprise you by throwing a life ring overboard without warning, so be prepared.

While you may practice man overboard recovery procedures again and again, realize there is no one way of coping with an overboard emergency. If there are two golden rules in larger yachts, they are to avoid starting the engine unless it is absolutely necessary, and to approach the victim from downwind.

It is essential you practice man overboard procedures any time you take off on a charter. Every yacht handles differently, and you should be aware of the differences before you need them in an emergency.

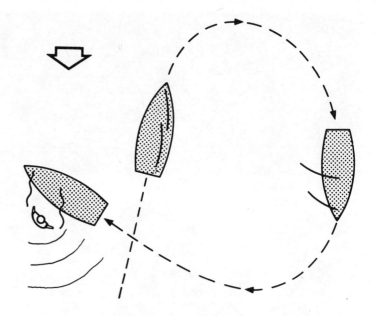

Figure 2-15 a *A quick jibe may be faster than some other available methods of recovering a person overboard.*

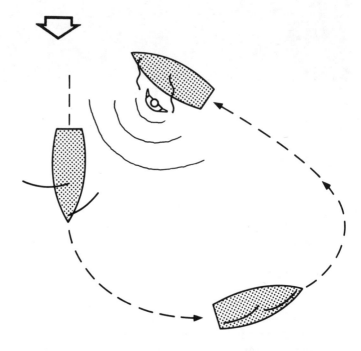

Figure 2-15 b *A sailboat running jibes one sail, heads up and tacks to get back to a person in the water. Both boats use a close reach approach to ensure the sails can luff or draw if necessary.*

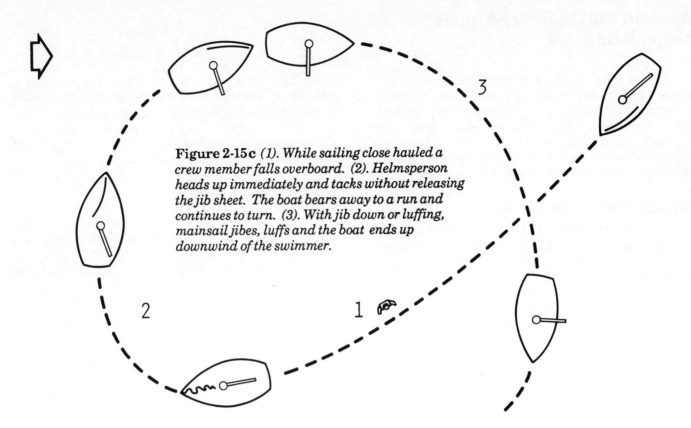

Figure 2-15c *(1). While sailing close hauled a crew member falls overboard. (2). Helmsperson heads up immediately and tacks without releasing the jib sheet. The boat bears away to a run and continues to turn. (3). With jib down or luffing, mainsail jibes, luffs and the boat ends up downwind of the swimmer.*

Quick Stop Method

The Man Overboard section of Sailing Fundamentals begins by saying that it is "One of the most hotly debated subjects in sailing...". In the Basic Sailing course, most instructors teach some variation of the "reach to reach" or "figure eight" method because beginners seem to have greater success with this type of system. Students are taught to sail away from the victim, then perform a tack and de-power the sails while returning to the swimmer. Panic usually accompanies an emergency and so the time used to sail away could actually help bring control to the boat. The skipper and crew could gain composure, thus increasing the chances of a safe recovery.

Two notable groups, The Seattle Sailing Foundation and the U. S. Naval Academy Sailing Squadron, have done extensive testing on another method, the "Quick Stop" man overboard recovery. Losing sight of the victim has proven to be one of the greatest problems preventing a successful recovery. Consider that only a person's head remains visible above the water's surface and even a small wave could obscure an object that size. The argument for sailing away to gain crew composure has become secondary to maintaining a fix on the swimmer. The Foundation and the Academy also determined that the longer a victim remained in the water, the less likely and more difficult a successful recovery became. Some experts consider returning as quickly as possible to be the highest priority and, thus, the "Quick Stop" method was born.

The Seattle Sailing Foundation concentrated primarily on short handed man overboard recovery using a device they market called the Lifesling. Readers are urged to contact the SSF, 7001 Seaview Ave. NW, Seattle, WA 98122 for details about the Lifesling. The diagram on this page concentrates on the process of returning. Both the Foundation and the Academy used the "Quick Stop" method.

Whenever someone goes overboard, a PFD should be thrown to them immediately. In the "Quick Stop", the boat is turned as soon as possible into, then through, the wind as if tacking. The jib would remain sheeted on the new windward side. The back-winding jib will help take some way off while turning the boat in a tighter circle. The boat will eventually bear away and jibe. By keeping the helm over, the boat repeats the process above. One or a series of small circles should allow the boat to return to the swimmer's location and render assistance. If the crew and situation will allow, dropping the jib to the deck will usually make the process flow more smoothly. The studies also found that stopping the boat to leeward worked more often than not.

More on the Charter Skipper's Responsibilities

Clearly, the skipper's primary responsibility is for the safety of crew and yacht , and for the condition of the vessel. This is a good moment in the course to add some other responsibilities, which may come into play just as soon as you go aboard. These are responsibilities of etiquette aboard and at anchor, which every crew member should know and obey.

Permission to Come Alongside

You are approaching a strange yacht in your dinghy, unannounced, perhaps to deliver a message, or to pick up a member of the crew. Common courtesy dictates that you hail her and ask for permission to come alongside. For all you know, another boat may be expected, or they are about to raise anchor. Best give the skipper the option to wave you off.

Permission to Come Aboard

When visiting another yacht, you should always ask for permission to come aboard. Once again, the skipper should have the option to ask you to come back later. Perhaps they are cleaning ship or having a meal, and are not ready for unexpected visitors.

Of course, there is no need to ask for permission when you have been invited to come over for a drink or for some other appointed purpose.

Right of First Arrival

In these days of congested charter areas and crowded anchorages, we sometimes forget the cardinal rule of courteous chartering: The first yacht to arrive has the right to the space to lie to her anchor or anchors in complete safety. Set your anchor, or secure alongside for that matter, in such a way that you do not infringe on her prior rights. The same rule applies to all yachts that have arrived before you.

By the same token, never lie to two anchors when everyone else is using one. If you do this, you will find that everyone else will swing into you.

Figure 2-16 *Common courtesy and the custom of the sea dictates that the first yacht to arrive has priority of anchorage.*

Figure 2-17 *Yacht displaying courtesy flag in proper position.*

Cruising and Racing

The cruising yacht should keep clear of yachts racing at all times, even if this means heaving to and waiting for the racers to pass. Identifying a racing fleet is easy near major ports. At sea, such vessels will usually advise you of their status when drawing close, perhaps even by VHF.

In narrow channels, move to one side of the channel until the racing fleet is past, anchoring if necessary.

The only time a cruising yacht takes precedence is when she is in distress.

Offering Assistance

Any yacht is obligated to render assistance to other vessels that are in distress or in need of help at sea. Nothing shall stand in the way of this responsibility, even if it is merely standing by while the yacht in trouble takes measures to correct the problem and even if it means many more hours at sea. **Someone else's problems at sea are always yours, too**, if you arrive on the scene and are in a position to render assistance.

At sea, one of the skipper's primary responsibilities is to avoid collisions with other vessels. To this end, you must be familiar with, and be able to apply, Regulations 1 to 19 of the International Regulations for the Prevention of Collision at Sea, otherwise known as 72 COLREGS. (The "72" refers to the year when the latest rules were adopted).
WE MOST STRONGLY URGE THAT YOU PURCHASE U.S. DEPARTMENT OF TRANSPORTATION U.S. COAST GUARD NAVIGATION RULES (COMDTINST16672.2A) 72 COLREGS 1 to 19.

Flag Etiquette

All too often, flag etiquette is perceived as being the province of elderly gentlemen in yachting caps and blazers. In fact, it is common courtesy to wear the appropriate flags in the correct places, especially when visiting a foreign country. Here are some general guidelines:

- **National flag**. This is worn on a flagstaff aft.
- **Courtesy flag**. This is the national flag of the country which you are visiting. You wear this at the starboard spreader, on the flag halyards provided. For example, in French waters like Martinique in the Caribbean, you would wear the national flag at the stern, the tricolor at the starboard spreader.
- **Burgee-house flag**. Time was when these were worn at the masthead, but the arrival of VHF radios and electronics has changed all this. You can wear them under the courtesy flag or on the flag halyards on the port spreader. If the matter of priority arises, the courtesy flag should be worn at the expense of the burgee-house flag.

Figure 2-18 *Buy these books.*

Every Naval and Merchant Marine deck officer knows COLREGS by heart. They have to navigate safely at sea. You should know the basics as well as they do. Rather than quote them in full, we summarize the main provisions for you.

We are concerned with Parts A and B of 72 COLREGS. Part A is entitled "General," and defines the terms of reference of the rules and key terms used throughout the regulations. Part B is the most important of all for the bareboater: "Steering and Sailing Rules".

Although several COLREGS were covered in your sailing fundamentals course, we make no apologies for covering the same ground again here. The rules are that important. We do, however, emphasize rules that are of particular importance to the bareboater.

Rules 1 to 3 constitute Part A, "General."

Rule 1 states that COLREGS apply to "all vessels on the high seas and in all waters connected therewith navigable by seagoing vessels." They can be overridden by official rules covering local waters, such as harbors, and ship lights can be modified by local governments. Special conditions can cause deviation from the rules to "avoid imminent danger ".

Rule 2 makes you, as skipper, responsible for the consequences of any failure to comply with COLREGS. In other words, you had better know the rules!

Rule 3 is concerned with definitions. For instance, a "vessel" includes hovercraft and seaplanes maneuvering on water. A "sailing vessel" is one under sail, not being propelled by its auxiliary engine. If, however, you switch on your motor, you are a "power-driven vessel" and subject to rules governing such craft.

A "vessel not under command" is a vessel that is unable to maneuver as required by COLREGS "through some exceptional circumstance." There is an important distinction between "not under command" and being a "vessel restricted in her ability to maneuver." These include vessels towing barges, dredgers, buoy tenders, minesweepers, and other specialized ships.

This is important if you charter in commercial harbors or near heavily traveled waters.

Rule 3 also defines "underway," "in sight of one another," and two important definitions for charter yachts:

"Restricted visibility." Conditions in which visibility is restricted by fog, mist, falling snow, heavy rain, or similar causes.

"Constrained by her draught." A power-driven vessel that is severely restricted in her ability to

maneuver because of available depth of water. This definition is important in harbor entrances and narrow channels.

Part B is divided into two parts, the first "The Conduct of Vessels," the second the actual sailing rules. It begins with **Rule 4**, which states that COLREGS apply in any visibility conditions.

Rule 5 enjoins a vessel to keep a good look out at all times, while **Rule 6** requires that "every vessel shall at all times proceed at a safe speed so that she can take proper and effective action to avoid collision and be stopped within a distance appropriate to the prevailing circumstances and conditions." "Safe speed" means taking into account visibility, traffic density, the presence of confusing background lights at night, vessel draught and depth of water.

Figure 2-19 *COLREGS Rule 6: A yacht proceeds at a "safe speed" in crowded waters.*

Rule 7 is vital to bareboaters navigating in crowded waters. It stresses that a vessel should assume that there is a risk of collision if she is uncertain if one does in fact exist. This rule uses one technique to define if the risk of collision exists: the use of bearings:

"Such risk shall be deemed to exist if the compass bearing of an approaching vessel does not appreciably change."

You should practice taking bearings on converging vessels at sea. Be aware, however, that COLREGS caution that very large ships or tows may be on a collision course even if the bearing does change. They are simply too large targets for conventional methods to apply.

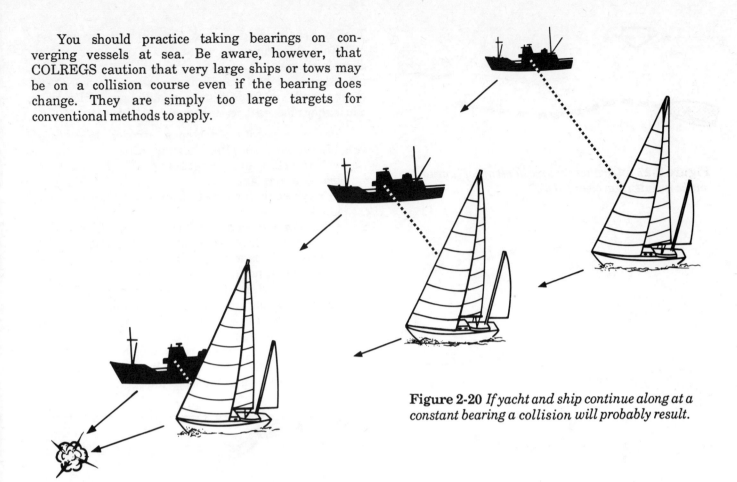

Figure 2-20 *If yacht and ship continue along at a constant bearing a collision will probably result.*

Rule 8 defines "actions to avoid collision." There are five important points here, summarized in the diagrams on the following page.

Rule 9 deals with narrow channels and fairways. It requires that you keep as close as is safe and prudent to the outer limit of the channel to your starboard side at all times. Most important to small boat sailors: a vessel less than 65 feet (20 meters) long "shall not impede the passage of a vessel that can safely navigate only within a narrow channel or fairway." You must not fish in a narrow channel, or cross in front of vessels with restricted ability to manuever. No anchoring in such places, and you are urged to use caution at narrow bends.

Whenever you overtake in a narrow channel, remember that the overtaking vessel is required to keep clear.

Rule 10 covers "Traffic Separation Schemes" and is of vital importance to the bareboater. These are traffic lanes, as it were, used in congested areas to separate shipping going in opposite directions.

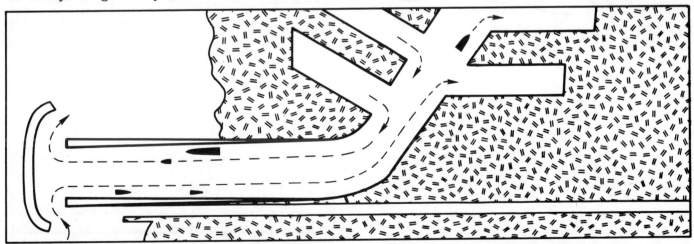

Figure 2-21 *Rule 9: Keep to the starboard side of the channel and out of the way of larger ships when they have restricted maneuverability.*

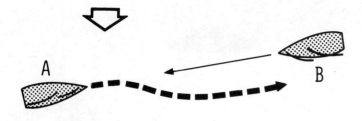

Figure 2-22 a *(A) alters course in plenty of time to make its intention clear to (B).*

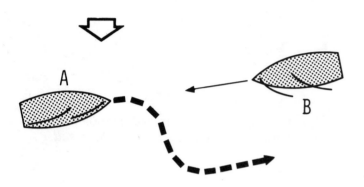

Figure 2-22 b *(A) alters course making a wide arc to assure (B) understands its intention.*

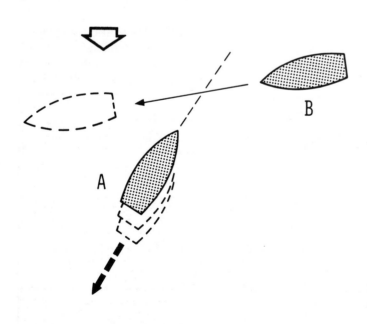

Figure 2-22 c *(A) engages reverse to slow the boat and allow (B) to claim its "stand-on" rights.*

Traffic Separation Schemes are in widespread use off the California coast, near New York, and major shipping arteries like the English Channel. They are identified by broad purple slashes on NOAA charts, and are important to small boat sailors because they place restrictions on your movement.

Traffic Separation schemes are for large vessels, but you must obey the following rules:
- If travelling in the direction of either lane, travel in that lane.
- Stay clear of the zone that separates the two lanes.
- Most important of all to yachts, cross all schemes as nearly as possible at right angles.
- If you join a lane, you should try and do so at its end, or at the shallowest possible angle.
- Most important of all, a vessel less than 65 feet (20 meters) long <u>or a sailing vessel</u> shall "not impede the safe passage of a power-driven vessel following a traffic lane."

Now the all-important rules which govern "The Conduct of Vessels in Sight of One Another," rules that apply to vessels in sight of one another.

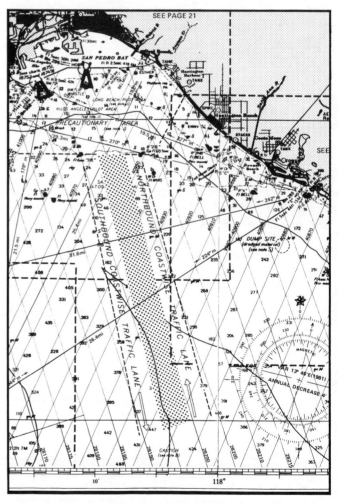

Figure 2-23 *Traffic Separation Zones are denoted by purple bands and dotted lines on NOAA charts.*

Rule 12: Sailing Vessels. This is the most important rule of all for a bareboat skipper. It deals with situations when two sailing vessels approach one another "so as to involve risk of collision."

Our diagram summarizes the basic definitions that apply to this rule, as well as port and starboard tack. Note that a sailing vessel is always deemed to be on either port or starboard tack.

Here are the major provisions of Rule 12:

When each has the wind on a DIFFERENT side, the vessel with the wind on the PORT side shall keep out of the way of the other.

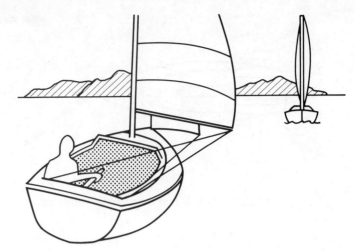

Figure 2-24 c *Steer clear of any vessel whose rights are not evident.*

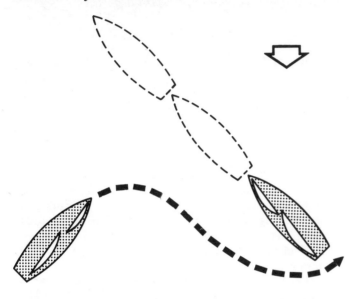

Figure 2-24 a *Starboard tack vessel is "stand-on" vessel.*

When both have the wind on the SAME side, the yacht to WINDWARD shall keep out of the way.

If the vessel with the wind on the PORT side sees another vessel to windward and cannot tell whether the other has the wind on port or starboard side, she keeps out of the way.

Note that the windward side is defined as the side OPPOSITE to that on which the mainsail is carried.

Yacht racing rules include somewhat different rules of the road, so keep clear of racing boats, as they may act according to those regulations without thinking of COLREGS.

Rule 13 is simplicity itself. An overtaking vessel always keeps out of the way of the craft being overtaken. You are an overtaking vessel when you are approaching from a direction more than 22.5 degrees abaft her beam. (This apparently strange angle is the legal angle aft of which you will see her stern light, but not her side lights, at night).

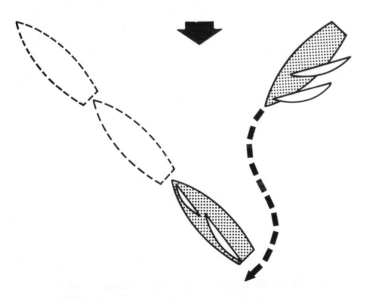

Figure 2-24 b *Windward vessel gives way to leeward vessel.*

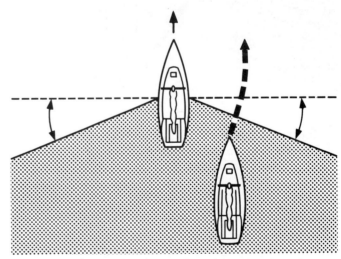

Figure 2-25 *Any vessel approaching within the shaded area (22.5 degrees abaft the beam) shall give way to the other vessel.*

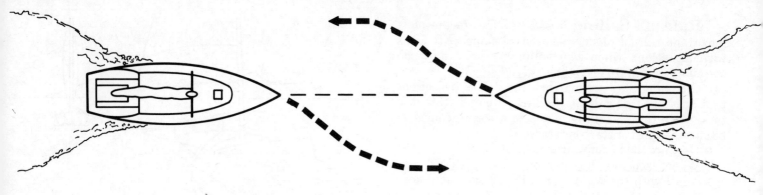

Figure 2-26. *When two vessels meet ,each alters course to starboard and they pass port to port.*

Rule 14 applies to you when you are under power.

When two power-driven vessels are approaching head on, each shall alter course to STARBOARD, so that they pass on the PORT side of the other.

Rule 15 is the crossing rule for power boats, and applied whenever your engine is running.

When two power-driven vessels are crossing and there is a risk of collision, the one that has the other on her STARBOARD side shall keep out of the way, and avoid crossing ahead of the other ship.

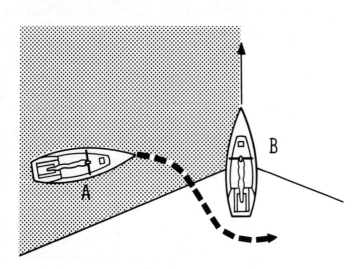

Figure 2-27 *A vessel (A) approaching within the "Danger Zone" (shaded area) must keep out of the way of the stand-on boat (B).*

Rule 16 is a simple statement to the effect that any vessel taking avoiding action should do so in good time, and in a "substantial" way.

Rule 17 covers the vessel that is "standing on" (not altering course). It adjures her to maintain course and speed, UNLESS it is apparent that the other ship is not complying with the rule, or when the actions of the latter are judged insufficient to avoid collision.

Rule 18 applies to both power and sailing vessels, as well as fishing boats and seaplanes. It is important to bareboaters, who often encounter sea planes, fishing boats, and dredgers. Sailing vessels are required to:
  • Keep out of the way of vessels not under command,
  • Keep out of the way of vessels constrained by their draught,
  • Fishing boats,
  • Vessels restricted in their ability to maneuver.
  • Power boats must additionally give way to sailing vessels. Remember that you are a power boat when you are using your diesel, even if your sails are set.

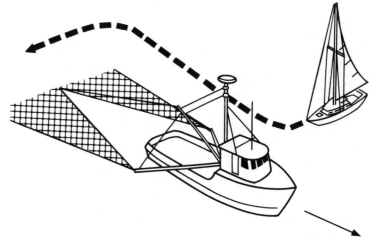

Figure 2-28 *Commercial fishing vessels with nets or dredges in the water should be allowed to pass at a considerable distance from pleasure boats.*

Subpart III of Section B consists of one rule, of paramount importance to anyone sailing in reduced visibility.

Rule 19 applies to every vessel not in sight of others, when operating in, or near, an area of restricted visibility. It requires every vessel to:

Proceed at a safe speed adapted to the prevailing circumstances.

Whenever a vessel in restricted visibility hears "apparently forward of her beam" the fog signal of another ship, or when she cannot avoid getting close to another vessel forward of her beam, she "shall reduce her speed to the minimum at which she can be kept on course." If necessary, she should take off all way.

By this time, you must be heartily sick of COLREGS. But we cannot stress too strongly just how important it is to know them thoroughly. You should be able to follow them instinctively on the water.

It is almost time to go on the water, but first let us learn two useful knots that will come in handy during your charter.

Trucker's Hitch

Sometimes called the Waggoner's Hitch, this is invaluable for lashing down loads, and provides a 2:1 purchase for applying strain. The Trucker's Hitch is simplicity itself.

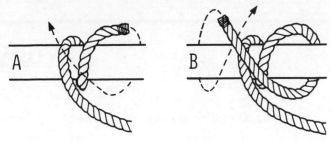

Figure 2-29

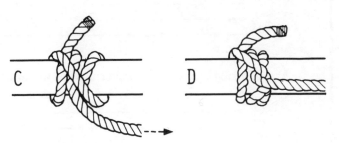

Rolling Hitch

The Rolling Hitch is an elaboration on that most useful of knots, the CLOVE HITCH, with the additional advantage that it can take strain at an angle. It is used to secure one line to another, or a rope to a spar. Rolling Hitches are invaluable when you want to move an anchor or dock line from one cleat to another. By securing another rope to a cleat and bending the other end to the line you want to move with a rolling hitch, you can take the strain with the knot while you move the bitter end in comfort.

Rolling hitches are most secure when the load is applied roughly parallel to the original rope.

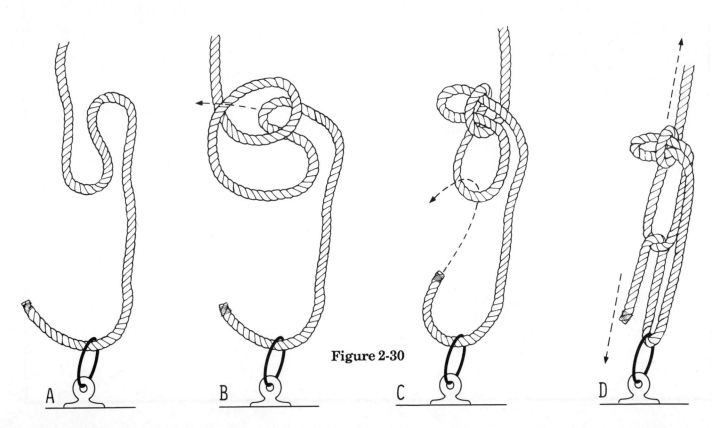

Figure 2-30

REVIEW QUESTIONS

1. List four items of sailing equipment and clothing that you need for a bareboat charter :

    a) _____

    b) _____

    c) _____

    d) _____

2. Describe two ways of recovering a crew member who has fallen overboard back on deck:

    a) _____

    b) _____

3. How would you cross a neighboring yacht rafted at a dock next to you:

    a) By the cockpit
    b) Over the cabin house
    c) Over the foredeck

4. Where do you fly the following flags on your charter yacht:

    a) The national flag: _____

    b) A courtesy flag: _____

5. You are under sail, and are on a collision course with a power-driven vessel coming straight towards you. Do you:

    a) Alter course to starboard
    b) Maintain course and speed
    c) Alter course to port

6. You are under sail with the wind on the starboard side. Another sailing vessel approaches on a collision course with the wind on the port side. Do you:

    a) Alter course
    b) Maintain course
    c) Lower sails and start the engine

7. You are in a narrow channel with 25 feet of water under power and see a large freighter approaching on a collision course in the middle of the deep water fairway. Do you:

    a) Maintain course and speed
    b) Alter course to the edge of the channel to keep out of her way
    c) Insist on your rights.

AFLOAT SKILLS

The afloat portion of this Section takes you into open water for your first sail. We practice hoisting and lowering sail, basic maneuvering of your charter yacht, man overboard drill, and some other fundamental seamanship skills.

The lesson begins with the yacht at the slip, sails bent on and halyards and sheets rigged ready for use. Acting as skipper, you start the engine, delegate crew members to ropes and fenders, and take the yacht out of the harbor under power. Remember to use the correct cruising speed under power and to obey harbor speed limits. Once you are clear of other vessels and have plenty of sea room, the instructor takes over and you are ready to set sail.

Hoisting Sail

Hoisting the mainsail is almost the same as it is in a smaller yacht, but here is a simple checklist:

1. **The skipper delegates crew members to specific tasks:**
   - One frees the main halyard from the winch and takes up the slack at the headboard.
   - One or two crew members release the sail ties that secure the mainsail to the boom.
   - One crew member slacks off the mainsheet, boom vang, and cunningham, so that the halyard can be used to take the weight of the boom as the sail is hoisted. The same person also checks that the reefing lines at the leach are running free.
2. **The skipper turns the bow of the boat into the wind,** keeping her stationary or moving ahead slowly under power.
3. **"Hoist main."** The sail is hoisted by hand, then with the aid of winch and winch handle, a second crew member tailing if necessary. Meanwhile, the other crew members check for snags, and the mainsheet hand slacks the sheet so that the sail flaps in the wind.
4. **"Slacken topping lift."** The weight of the boom has been taken by the topping lift until now. Slackening it means the sail assumes its correct shape. (Many yachts have self adjusting topping lifts, which means you can ignore this instruction).
5. **"Trim."** The mainsheet hand trims the sail. As soon as it fills, the skipper checks the set, the wrinkles along the luff and foot. Some adjustments with halyard, cunningham, and sail outhaul may be necessary.
6. **The skipper throttles back the engine and turns it off,** while the crew coil the halyard and loop it over the cleat.
   Once the main is setting nicely, it is time for the jib. Since setting a hanked jib is identical on small and large vessels, we will confine our remarks to roller furlers.

Figure 2-31 *The mainsail supports the boom while underway sailing.*

1. The skipper delegates crew members to:
   - **Prepare the lee jib sheet.** Take a wrap on the winch. However, they do not use the winch until the sail is unrolling smoothly. If there are enough people, one crew member will crank the winch handle, the other haul and tail.
   - **Slacken out the jib control line** as the sail unrolls. The delegated hand uncoils the line and makes sure it will run out smoothly.
2. **"Set jib."** The sheet crew haul in on the leeward sheet, checking that the weather sheet is running free. The sail begins to unroll faster and faster as the wind catches it. Meanwhile, the hand on the control line looks out for snags and lets the rope run forward smoothly, so that there are no snarls on the drum up forward. Once the unfurling is well under way, the winch crew set up the sheet on the winch drum and haul in, without, however, placing great strain on the line sheet until the sail is fully unfurled.
3. Once the sail is fully unfurled, the winch crew trim it under the skipper's supervision.

NEVER USE A SHEET WINCH TO UNROLL A ROLLER-FURLING JIB. YOU WILL TEAR THE SAIL OR DAMAGE THE FURLING MECHANISM.

If the sail fails to unfurl, check for mechanical malfunction or control line mis-feeding.

Figure 2-32

Staysail

The routine for hoisting the staysail is exactly the same as that for the jib, except that the sheet hand will probably be dealing with a self-tending sail (see above).

We are now sailing along nicely on a beam reach, and it is time to familiarize ourselves with a larger sailing vessel.

Figure 2-33 *Charter vacations are not endurance tests. Smart sailors recruit plenty of help for chores.*

Basic Sailing in a Larger Yacht

The first thing to remember is that everything moves much slower in a large charter yacht. No 40-footer spins like a top, not even the fastest light displacement racing boat. Everything happens that bit slower, which is a good thing. It gives you time to think ahead.

For the next 20 minutes, you become accustomed to the bulk of the yacht, first on a beam reach, then hard on the wind.

Once you have stayed on one tack for a while, come about. Tacking is exactly the same, except that the boat turns slower through the eye of the wind. Since the yacht is much larger, you should be careful to assign strong crew members to crank in on the sheet winches. Most charter yachts have two speed, self tailing winches. You start by cranking with high gearing, then simply change down to a lower gear by cranking in the opposite direction. This makes sail trimming much easier.

When tacking a larger yacht, coming about takes longer, so you will have time to crank in much of the jib sheet before the wind fills the sail. If you can, take your time swinging, so that you make things easier on the crew.

If the yacht is stuck in IRONS (in the eye of the wind), backwind or keep the jib on its original side so that it fills aback. This will turn the bow onto the new tack. When you are sure she is going to make it, let the sheet go, and crank in on the new side.

After a while on the opposite tack, the instructor will tell you to turn downwind, to practice running. This enables you to try jibing and setting the jib wing-and-wing.

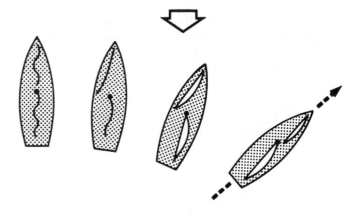

Figure 2-34 *As sailboat bears away from the wind with the jib sheeted to weather, the sail helps push the bow in the right direction.*

Jibing

Jibing is potentially the most dangerous maneuver carried out under sail because the main boom comes across with considerable force perhaps, if you are not careful, without warning. This can be dangerous in a small vessel, but the danger is magnified many times on a charter yacht of 40-foot or more.

Here is a sequence of events for a downwind jibe. You are running with the wind blowing from the port side, with the mainsail boomed out to starboard and the genoa on the same side.

"Stand by to Jibe"

Two crew members are assigned to the jib sheets, as with coming about. A third person mans the main sheet. If there are only two crew members, priority should be given to handling the main. Sheets are uncleated, and coils checked to see they are running clear. The difference with a large yacht is that one hand deals with the mainsail as a full-time job.

Figure 2-35 *Careful control of the mainsheet is essential when jibing a larger yacht.*

"Jibe-Ho!"

1. **The skipper turns the wheel to port** in a steady turn, not too fast, but so that there is adequate boat control.
2. As the yacht turns, **the mainsail hand hauls in the mainsheet** hand-over-hand until it is almost hard-in and the boom is amidships.
3. The jib sheet crew **slacken off and haul in sheets** as they would when going about. The sail will come over faster, however, and a smart crew will maintain control as it slats across.

Figure 2-36 *A spinnaker pole may double as a whisker pole on a charter yacht.*

4. As the boom swings onto the starboard side, the mainsheet hand eases out the sheet smoothly and smartly, easing the shock of the jibe and the heeling motion that goes with it. When things have settled down, the mainsail is trimmed for the new course.
   Practice this several times, until the maneuver is smooth and second nature.

Wing and Wing (Winging Out the Jib)

This exercise is carried out exactly the same way as it is on a small boat, except that the whisker pole (often a spinnaker pole) has a topping lift, and perhaps a downhaul or foreguy as well. Since the gear is a little more complicated than on a smaller vessel, we cover it in detail here. Let us go through the exercise, with the yacht running downwind with the wind dead astern, and the jib blanketed behind the main on the starboard side.

1. Remove the WHISKER POLE from its chocks on the foredeck, by pulling the release wires for the pins.
2. Attach the inboard end (normally the ends are interchangable) to the spinnaker boom ring on the forward side of the mast. Rest the other end on the foredeck to windward.
3. Unhook the spinnaker pole topping lift from its normal home on the spinnaker pole ring.
   Attach it to the ring on the lift wire that suspends the pole at the midpoint.

4. Insert the loose windward jib sheet into the outboard fitting on the pole as it lies on the deck.

5. Haul the pole off the deck with the topping lift until it is horizontal. Rig a downhaul to the deck from the midpoint of the pole if necessary.

6. Haul in the windward jib sheet, so the sail sets on the pole on the windward side, giving you a wing and wing rig. Unrigging the whisker pole is simplicity itself:

1. Slacken the topping lift and jib sheet, and pull on the outboard piston release wire as the sheet comes forward.

2. Take control of the jib on the other side with the sheet.

3. Lower the pole to the deck and stow topping lift and spar.

Heaving-to

Much of this lesson is taken up with getting the feel of handling a large yacht in open water. Along the way, take every opportunity to practice COLREGS under actual sailing conditions.

There is one invaluable maneuver that you may use again and again when chartering, especially when reefing in open water, or when you want to wait for a squall to pass. Perhaps, too, you may want to stop in open water to cook a meal, rest, or wait for a tide to turn. This is heaving-to, bringing the yacht to a complete stop under sail.

You learned this maneuver in your basic course, but let us go through the procedure once again:

1. **Bring the yacht hard on the wind,** close-hauled on either port or star-board tack and settle down at cruising speed.

2. "Heave-to." **The skipper puts the yacht about** onto the other tack, <u>but no one touches the jib sheets</u>. The boat comes round, and the jib fills in the aback position.

3. **The skipper turns the helm back in the direction of the wind** once the boat has tacked over.

4. You are now "hove-to." However, you will have to adjust the sail plan against the rudder, which is hard over, so that the vessel remains station-

ary. You use the mainsail for this purpose, sheeting in or slacking the main until you reach the correct balance of sailplan to keep you as stationary as possible. Once this is done, the vessel should forereach very slightly, drifting as little as possible to leeward. The skipper lashes the helm hard over. Except for keeping a sharp lookout, you can go below, cook a meal, prepare an anchor, reef, or carry out whatever tasks you need to complete.

You should always heave-to with plenty of sea room, as the yacht can drift a considerable distance, especially in strong winds. Heaving-to is a useful maneuver, especially when the crew is tired and needs some rest in rough water. You will be astonished at the difference it makes.

Bareboaters and cruising sailors generally tend to use heaving-to more than small boats, so they have to be aware when NOT to do so. **Do not heave-to in:**

- Restricted waters, except for a very short time when changing sails, etc, and then only out of narrow channels,
- Shipping lanes,
- Fishing grounds,
- Traffic separation zones.

To start sailing again:

1. **The skipper mans the wheel,** assigning two crew members to the jib sheets.

2. "Let Draw." **The skipper brings the wheel close to amidships,** ready to steer ahead. The jib hands let go the windward jib sheet and haul in on the leeward one as fast as they can. The skipper sets the new course as the yacht gathers steerage way.

3. **Trim sails for the new course.**

Steering a Compass Course

A great deal of bareboating involves passage-making, setting compass courses that you will follow for hours. It is time for us to familiarize ourselves with steering a compass course, so that you know what to do when on passage.

Remove the BINNACLE COVER (compass cover) and refresh your memory about the COMPASS CARD, the numerical points that are usually marked every 5 degrees, and find the LUBBER LINE, the vertical mark aligned with the bow of the boat that provides the mark for steering your course by. The course indicated by the compass and lubber line is sometimes called the SHIP'S HEADING.

Next take the helm and set the yacht on a beam reach heading toward a convenient landmark a-shore. Once the sails are trimmed correctly:

1. **Steer for the landmark** and settle the vessel on course.
2. Once you are moving at a steady speed and have the feel of the boat, **look down at the lubber line.** The number on the compass card OPPOSITE the lubber line is your compass course.
3. **Now steer the yacht by compass course,** using the movements of the compass card to adjust your course. Do not look at the landmark, but keep a lookout for other boats. Use the wheel to keep the boat on course, making as few movements of the rudder as you can.

Now alter course to ... degrees. Move the wheel to port or starboard to bring the lubber line round to that particular ship's head. Once you reach the setting, adjust the wheel to steady the boat on the new course.

You will repeat this exercise two or three times, while the crew adjust the sails for the new course. At least one of these maneuvers will involve going about or jibing, so that you get used to altering courses from one compass heading to another.

This exercise will end with the yacht heading offshore toward a bare horizon, with no land ahead of you. It is time to practice steering a compass course without landmarks to check against.

1. **Choose a course to steer.** Let us say it is 220 degrees Magnetic.
2. Use the wheel to **bring the vessel round to the correct heading.**
3. **Trim sails** for the course to be followed.
4. **Steer the vessel on 220 degrees** looking at the compass every few seconds until she settles down.
5. Once you have the feel of the boat, ask a crew member to time you.
6. **Now steer the course** WITHOUT LOOKING AT THE COMPASS for 30 seconds. After 30 seconds, look at the compass and make corrections if necessary. Repeat the exercise several times, lengthening the period when you watch the horizon until it reaches 2 minutes.

By this time, you should have a good feel for steering a compass course. Chances are you are carrying out this exercise in relatively smooth water. Following compass courses is considerably harder in rougher water, when you have to compensate for wave action, but this is a matter of practice, which you will acquire on charter.

Figure 2-38 *Recognizable landmarks make the helmsperson's job easier.*

Lowering Sail

Once you are competent at sailing a compass course, set a final compass course for the harbor. Once you have sailed close enough to the entrance, it is time to lower sail and enter port under power.

Lowering sail follows a simple routine, a routine slightly different from smaller yachts, for you have heavier sails and a topping lift to be concerned with:

1. **Start the engine** and warm it up.
2. **Engage forward** and steer the boat slowly head-to-wind in a place where there is adequate sea room, clear of harbor traffic.
3. **Assign crew members to:**
   - man main and jib halyards
   - gather jib on deck if it is not a roller-jib
   - gather main and stow same on the boom with ties
   - handle jib and main sheets.
4. **"Lower jib."** Jib sheets are slackened, jib halyard cast off, and jib gathered onto the foredeck, where it is secured temporarily for later removal from the forestay. If the jib is a roller-furler, then the crew haul in on the jib control line, easing the sheet carefully as they do so.
5. **"Check topping lift."** The halyard hand mans the topping lift and takes the weight of the boom on the lift. The main sheet is slack while this operation is carried out. It is then tightened to secure the boom if necessary..
6. **"Lower main."** The mainsheet is hauled hard in as the main halyard is cast off. The halyard hand pulls down the sail at the gooseneck, while the crew gather in the body of the main.
7. Mainsail is stowed on the boom either by rolling or folding, according to the system used on the individual yacht.
8. Once everything is secure, the skipper alters course for harbor under power.

You now power back to the slip, ending Section 2 of the course. We have already covered the skills needed for entering a slip under power, so you can end the lesson by practicing them again.

Section 3 builds on the skills in the previous two sections, and gives you a more advanced lesson in the care and handling of a diesel auxiliary engine.

Figure 2-39

SECTION 3

ENGINES
AND
MANEUVERING UNDER POWER

ASHORE KNOWLEDGE

So far, we have explored the basic features of the charter yacht, carried out some basic maneuvers under power, and learned some fundamentals about handling a larger yacht under sail. This section returns to the engine, the diesel power unit that you will use frequently on your charter. The Ashore Knowledge section looks at the engine itself, at some of the routine maintenance you should undertake every day, and weekly. Then we discuss some of the common problems that can develop with a hard-worked diesel, and how you can diagnose and correct them. After that, we take the yacht into open water and learn some very important techniques for handling your vessel under power.

Exploring the Engine

In Section I, we described the engine control panel and starting controls, which are usually within reach of the helm, so they can be operated from the cockpit. Before exploring the engine itself, just refresh your memory as to the position and features of these items.

• The ENGINE CONTROL PANEL usually contains the IGNITION KEY and the OIL AND BATTERY WARNING LIGHTS. There are dials that indicate oil pressure, water temperature, and battery charging rate as well. This is where the panel switch that illuminates these dials is also located.

• The DECOMPRESSION LEVER for stopping the engine usually forms part of the control panel, or is found close by.

• THROTTLE and GEAR CONTROLS are usually located on the WHEEL PEDESTAL, close to the helm. In some cases the throttle doubles as the decompression switch when pushed to its absolute minimum level.

• The FUEL GAUGE is sometimes found below near the main electrical control panel, or is part of, or near, the engine control panel.

• The MAIN BATTERY SWITCH lies near the main electrical control panel.

Be sure to locate all these controls before opening up the engine. Be sure, too, to practice starting and stopping the engine so that it is second nature. We shall assume you know this from this moment on.

Figure 3-1 *The engine control panel will usually be located in the cockpit near the wheel and controls.*

Engine Access

In most charter yachts, the engine is located under the cockpit. Sometimes it lies amidships, under the galley area. The engine is hidden from sight, behind sound-proofed hatches in the cockpit floor or under the main companionway. Aft cockpit vessels often have a passage that connects the salon and aft cabins below decks; in this case you can gain access to the diesel through doors in the side of the passage. To gain access to the engine, you must first remove the hatches that conceal it.

1. **Remove engine access** hatch in the floor of the cockpit. This may hinge out of the way, or be completely removable. This will give you access to the engine from above.
   Some yachts have their engines set well forward, so you have access from the front and side. In this instance, the access from the cockpit will probably be through one of the cockpit lockers.

2. Now **remove the companionway steps** and put them out of the way in the salon. You can now draw back the bolts that hold the engine cover in place and lift it out of the way. This gives you access to the forward facing parts of the engine, especially the alternator and alternator belts.

In the case of a large yacht, or one with a side passage below decks, you will probably enjoy the luxury of a separate engine room. This is accessible from the side, but sometimes also from the cockpit. As a general rule, it is best to give yourself as much light and space as possible, so you can get at the engine from every angle.

Engine Anatomy

Almost every charter yacht has a diesel engine, not a power unit that most automobile owners are familiar with. But the diesel is ideal for any yacht. It uses low flashpoint fuel, which reduces the risk of fire, is highly economical, and is highly reliable. With proper care and regular oil changes, a yacht diesel will give trouble-free service for years. Of course, charter yachts' diesels are worked far harder than those of privately owned yachts. But they still give remarkably reliable service.

At first glance, the engine that emerges from under the hatches may seem unfamiliar and confusing. There are no spark plugs or carburetors. In fact, the engine is simplicity itself. Let us take a short tour of its major components, especially the ones that you should examine regularly.

Starting at the forward end of the unit:

• ALTERNATOR. Now look for the belt that runs from the flywheel to the alternator. This provides electrical charge for the battery and for the engine itself. The tension of these belts is especially important for proper battery charging.

• HEAT EXCHANGER. Fresh water component of the engine cooling system with radiator cap. Some boats have a purely salt water system.

• WATER PUMP. This pump operates the salt water cooling system and is normally located on the side of the engine. Your instructor will show you the water impeller housing, for this is the part you may have to replace if you have overheating problems during your charter.

Figure 3-2

• INJECTORS. The injectors, set in the cylinder head, are the devices that monitor the amount of diesel fuel that goes to the cylinders. They are joined by thin metal pipes to the INJECTOR PUMP. This is the nerve system of the diesel engine. Both injectors and the injector pump are basically sealed units as far as you are concerned. They need specialized tools for even routine adjustment, tools that only a diesel workshop or charter company will own. Locate the FUEL PUMP with its manual lever on the side of the engine. You may need this for bleeding the fuel system (see photo).

One important point about diesel engines; their fuel systems require <u>absolutely airtight joints and clean fuel</u>. The slightest impurity or air bubble causes immediate problems. With a diesel, cleanliness is certainly next to godliness...

Figure 3-3b *Fuel filter and lines.*

• FUEL FILTERS. Although diesel pumps at a service station usually provide clean fuel, your engine has not only a built-in fuel filter, but additional ones in the fuel line. These are normally located on the side of the engine compartment. They are glass or plastic units, with the filters contained in the bowl, the fuel lines passing in and out of the top. The sediment caught by the filters falls to the bottom of the bowl and is easily drained away or cleaned out.

• OIL DIP STICK. Like all engines, your diesel needs oil to lubricate its innards. All yacht diesels have dip sticks, just like your car. Locate the stick, which lies on one side of the engine or the other. It may take you a few moments to find this with the confined space and plethora of wires surrounding the power unit. The loop is often painted red.

Pull it out of its housing and wipe it clean with a rag or paper towel. You will see two lines, just like those on your car's stick. The engine oil level should be between them. Replace the stick and test the oil level just like you would do in your garage.

Figure 3-3c *Oil dip stick.*

•OIL FILTER AND FILLER. The oil filter is just like that on your car, and usually located close to the dip stick. Find it, so that you at least know where it is. The oil filler cap is to be found on top of the engine. This is where you add oil should the dip stick level be low. The charter company will normally provide the oil, usually diesel grade 10W/30 or /40.

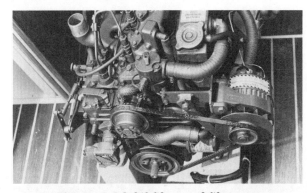

Figure 3-3d *Oil filter and filter cap.*

• STARTER MOTOR. This is a sealed unit with its SOLENOID. Should you be unlucky enough to have starter motor trouble, it may be due to loose wiring, which you can tighten easily. If the trouble is any worse, the unit will have to be replaced with a new one. Since you are most unlikely to be carrying a spare starter motor, the company will have to cope with the problem.

Figure 3-3e *Starter motor.*

Figure 3-3f *Transmission oil is checked and added here.*

• TRANSMISSION DIP STICK AND FILLER. The transmission lies just aft of the engine and requires its own lubricant. The transmission oil level is checked with its own dip stick in the top of the box, and oil is added through the same orifice. Locate the transmission box and the stick. It is unlikely, however, that you will have to add oil to the transmission during your brief charter. Again, the charter company will provide the necessary transmission oil, usually 30 weight.

Figure 3-3g *Stuffing box.*

• STUFFING BOX AND STERN GLAND. The PROPELLOR SHAFT extends aft from the transmission box and leaves the hull through the stern gland aft. A slight drip of seawater should be visible. It is necessary for lubrication of the gland, so there is a large stern gland nut or stuffing box that has to be tightened, and occasionally be repacked. Locate this gland. You are unlikely to have to touch this unless a serious leak develops. In this case, the charter company will come out and service it.

• ENGINE SEACOCKS. These bring salt water in for engine cooling and carry it away when its work is done. Locate the positions of these cocks, and learn how to open and close the valves, whether they are gates or screw-down types. There are often valves on the exhaust pipe and engine cooling water intake that should be located, just in case you have to shut them under sail in rough weather.

The intake sea cock will have a simple trap on it to catch kelp, grass, and other debris. You should locate this, and know how to remove it for <u>cleaning, in case the engine overheats.</u>

<u>To remove an</u> intake cleaner for cleaning:

1. **Close sea cock.**
2. **Unscrew glass or plastic filter holder**.
3. **Remove filter** or trap inside and clean thoroughly.
4. **Replace filter and holder,** screw down tight, reopen sea cock.

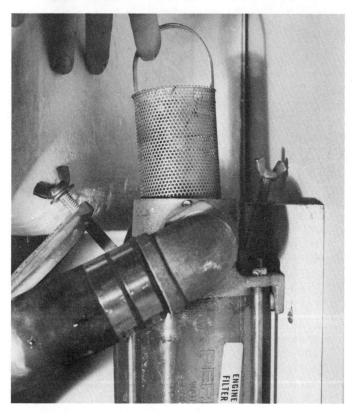

Figure 3-4 *Water intake filter during cleaning.*

• FUEL FILLER CAP. Many people go off on charter without locating the fuel filler cap. This normally lies on deck somewhere near the cockpit. Ensure that you know where it is, and also the tool used to open it.

<u>Be sure to distinguish between the deck fillers for diesel fuel, water, and holding tanks. They are normally clearly marked.</u>

Safety and Your Engine

Diesels are about the safest engines you can ship out with, but there are some elementary precautions that should always be followed:

- **Never smoke** when refuelling or working on the engine.

- **Never lean over the exposed engine with loose clothing** when the unit is running. You could catch yourself in the flywheel or alternator belts. By the same token, never put your fingers near moving parts when the engine is running.

- If the cockpit lockers open into the engine compartment, **check that no items of gear are overflowing** into it, which can interfere with moving parts.

- After working on the engine, check that you have cleared away any loose rags or tools, and that the engine covers are securely fastened.

Routine Maintenance

The secret to trouble-free engines is regular maintenance. As a charterer, your responsibilities are relatively limited, but extremely important for all that. Routine checking of certain items will minimize the chances of a breakdown during your trip.

Daily Checklist

Daily, before lifting anchor or casting off, check the following:

- **Engine oil level** with the dip stick. Add oil if necessary.

- **Alternator belts** are correctly tensioned. The charter company will tell you what is correct.
Normally, an adjustment will be unnecessary, as this is checked before you set out on your charter.

- **Fuel level.**

- **Water level** in heat exchanger is correct. Top off if necessary.

- **Check sea cocks are open.**

Then start the engine and let it warm up for a few minutes. Now check:

- **Oil pressure level** is within acceptable range. This range is defined in the engine instructional manual - the charter company will tell you what figures to use.

- **Batteries** are charging properly.

Figure 3-5 *Take extra care to tuck in loose clothing and tie hair while working on an engine that is running.*

- **Engine temperature** is within acceptable range.

If any of these readings are unsatisfactory, stop the engine, diagnose, and correct the problem before starting up again.

- Look over the side and check if **water is coming out of the exhaust outlet**.

- Quickly check **gear and throttle controls** for correct operation, while still anchored or at the slip.

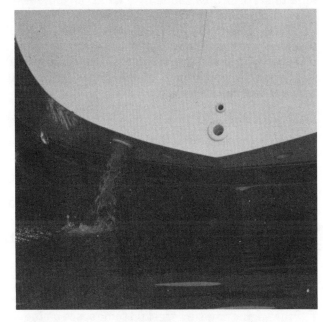

Figure 3-6 *Always check water discharge with exhaust.*

Weekly Checklist

The same as for daily, with the addition of:

• **Battery water levels** should be at right level. Top off if necessary.

• **Check transmission fluid level.**

• **Engine water intake filter** should be clean. Remove and clear if necessary.

• Inspect **fuel filters** and clean bowls if necessary.

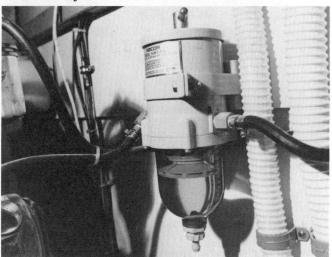

Figure 3-7 *Fuel filters are usually easily accessible for cleaning.*

TROUBLE SHOOTING

You are ready to take off, or are enjoying a comfortable passage under power, when the engine fails to start or dies suddenly. What do you do? Can you trouble-shoot and fix the problem?

Take heart! 95 percent of all diesel engine troubles are simplicity itself to diagnose and fix, provided you trace the trouble simply and logically. Let us go through some of the important potential troubles that can afflict you.

Engine Fails to Start

Other than a defective starter motor, there are two basic causes for failure to start — lack of electrical power or a fuel malfunction. Let us break these causes down a little further:

If the engine fails to turn over, or is hesitant to do so, your problem is probably an electrical one.

1. **Check that the Main Battery Switch** is on BOTH. If it is not, switch it there and try starting again. Then try BATT. 1 and BATT.2 separately.
2. If this fails, **pull out the Decompression lever.** If the engine now turns, get up some speed on the crankshaft, then push in the lever. The engine may fire.

Should this trick work, run the engine for a considerable time to charge batteries, and check for obvious causes of non-charging, such as slack alternator belts or low water levels in the batteries.

3. You are still stuck. **Check the battery terminals** for tightness, and clean them so there is a good connection. **Check water levels** in the batteries.
4. Should the engine still not start, **check for loose wires** on the starter motor. Tighten them with care and try again. It is amazing how often this is the problem.

If none of these remedies work, then you have dead batteries, or a problem like a defunct starter motor or alternator.

In the event your batteries ARE dead:

• **Take them ashore** and have them checked by a service station. If they are capable of holding charge, have them reactivated. If not, call the charter company about replacements.

• If you are in an anchorage away from facilities, try and **find a yacht with jumper cables** aboard to start you. If this works, check belt tension and other obvious reasons for lack of charge as the engine runs.

• **Call the charter company.** They will ask you a set of questions that will basically take you through the procedures listed above. If these do not work, they will send out someone to fit a new alternator or starter motor, or to fix whatever problem is causing the malfunction, or suggest an appropriate solution.

Some smaller engines can be turned over manually with a starting handle. If your yacht is of this type, necessary instructions will be found in the engine area.

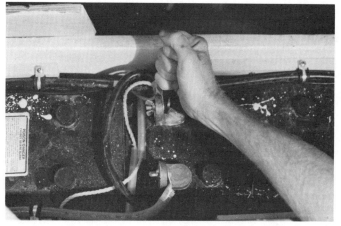

Figure 3-8 *Loose or dirty battery cable ends may prevent the engine from starting.*

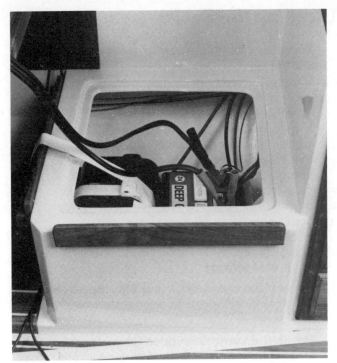

Figure 3-9 *Cables leading from another yacht can be used to jump dead batteries.*

If the Engine Turns Over Normally, But Fails to Fire:

1. If the engine is equipped with a pre-heater, **try pre-heating the engine again,** especially if it is cold. If this does not work:

2. **Check the fuel level** in the tank. It is amazing how often this is the problem. Bleed the fuel system and proceed (see page 58).
If your yacht has two fuel tanks, check levels in both and switch to the fuller tank. Bleed system if necessary.

3. **Check the injector piping** for leaks and tighten any joints displaying traces of fuel spillage or air bubbles. Then bleed system.

4. **Check fuel filters.** If they are excessively dirty, clean them, bleed system, and try again.

5. **Listen for electric fuel pumps** if so equipped. A loose wire or fuse leading to the fuel pump could cause it to malfunction.

If none of these procedures work, call the charter company. You may have either injector problems or a malfunctioning injector pump, both troubles beyond your capability to repair. Very occasionally, the exhaust system may siphon sea water into your cylinder head. The charter company may ask you to check this by removing an injector and inspecting the head, but do NOT do this without them asking you to.

Alternator Charge Light Comes On

This means the alternator is not charging the batteries.

1. STOP ENGINE AT ONCE

2. **Check tension of alternator belts.** Adjust if necessary.

3. **Check for loose wires** on alternator and batteries. Tighten if necessary.

4. **Check wiring and globe at alternator light.** Replace if necessary.

5. If none of these procedures work, call the charter company. Your alternator is probably defective.

Figure 3-10 *After loosening the bolts which hold the alternator in place, one hand pries the alternator away from the engine while the other tightens the bolts.*

Engine Overheats

You should look at the water temperature level on the engine control panel every five minutes or so. If the engine is overheating and the temperature needle is above 190 to 225 deg. F.

1. STOP ENGINE AT ONCE TO AVOID DAMAGE. Never run an overheated engine, for you can do irreparable damage in minutes.

2. **Let engine cool.** While it is, check engine seacocks are open. Check engine intake filter and clean if necessary. This is a very common problem, but one often forgotten.

3. **Check intake and exhaust hoses** for leaks and damage, also hose clamps. Tighten and replace if necessary. When engine is cooled down, check water level in heat exchanger and top off if necessary.

Figure 3-11 *Once the impeller cover has been located and removed, the impeller should come free with a little prying. A snap ring may hold impeller on the shaft.*

4. **Check water pump impeller** and change if necessary. Proceed as follows:

   a. **Unscrew impeller cover,** lay screws and lid aside carefully.

   b. **Remove cover gasket** very carefully, so it can be reused. If in doubt replace with spare aboard.

   c. Carefully **lever out the damaged impeller** with one or two screwdrivers.

   d. **Clean the housing and fit a new impeller.**

   e. **Replace gasket and lid** and screw tight.

If these procedures do not work, call the charter company.

These are practically all the troubles you may encounter with your diesel short of a major sieze up or malfunction that is simply an Act of God. With that sort of problem, all you can do is to sail your boat to port and call the experts.

Bleeding the Fuel System

There is something faintly intimidating about a diesel that makes "bleeding the fuel system" seem awesomely difficult. It is not, indeed many newer engines have automatic bleeding systems, so you do not have to worry.

Diesel fuel systems give trouble if there is air in the pipes. Bleeding removes these air pockets and ensures a steady flow of fuel.

You bleed your engine when it runs out of fuel — which is why you should try and avoid running dry, when you have cleaned the filters, or removed the injectors for servicing. Here is the procedure:

1. Complete repairs or fill fuel tank. **Turn on fuel** if this is necessary.

2. **Loosen the nut closest to the pump** where one of the injector pipes joins the injector at the cylinder head.

3. **Pump the manual lever** on the fuel pump until all air bubbles are pushed out of the pipe and pure fuel flows steadily. If fuel pump is electrical, activate same with ignition switch until same effect is achieved.

4. **Tighten nut.**

5. **Continue process** to furthest injector.

6. **Start engine normally.**

Figure 3-12 *Injector nuts should be loosened one by one.*

WHAT TO DO IF YOUR ENGINE STOPS UNDER WAY

If your engine stops when you are under way, you immediately lose way and will soon be dead in the water unless you set sail. If you have plenty of sea room and are outside shipping lanes, you can take your time setting sail, or simply remain stationary in the water until repairs are completed. But what do you do if you are in congested waters or shipping lanes?

Your Engine Fails in a Crowded Anchorage or Confined Waters

If there is time and there is a breeze, set sail immediately, and sail out of the fairway or congested water until you can anchor safely. A rolling jib will help you set sail quicker.

In calm weather, if in shallow water, anchor immediately. If repairs cannot be made at once, tow the vessel out of the fairway to safety with the dinghy, or with the help of another yacht.

If this is impracticable, raft temporarily up against a nearby vessel until you can get the engine running or tow clear.

Always have crew members with fenders ready if your engine fails in congested waters.

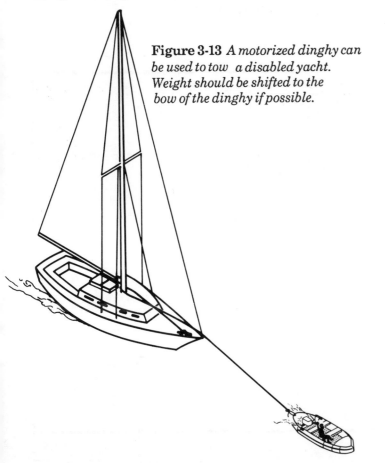

Figure 3-13 *A motorized dinghy can be used to tow a disabled yacht. Weight should be shifted to the bow of the dinghy if possible.*

The most dangerous situations are those where you experience engine failure in foggy or calm weather in the middle of a shipping lane. Under these circumstances **set your radar reflector immediately and sound the correct fog signals.** Try and tow your vessel clear of the shipping lane with the dinghy, if you have one, while effecting repairs as soon as possible. Your safest strategy is to anchor in shallow water if this is possible, in a place where fast moving, large vessels cannot collide with you.

TOOLS AND SPARES

Every charter yacht carries a toolkit and some essential spare parts for the diesel — and, for that matter, for such pieces of equipment as the stove and the toilet. It is well that you know what items are common in such kits.

Toolkit

The responsibility for providing a toolkit with adequate tools lies with your charter company. However, the following tools are useful. You may care to take some of your own along with you:

Hammer
Vise grips
Adjustable wrenches
Set of socket wrenches
Set of crescent wrenches
Allen wrenches
Screwdrivers — slot and Philips, of at least two sizes
Wire cutters
Circuit tester
Hacksaw and spare blades

Spare Parts

Duct tape
Ripstop tape for sail repairs
Some fine nylon line
Sail repair kit
Water pump impeller kit
Alernator belts
Engine hoses
Hose clamps of correct size
Assortment of shackles
Siezing wire
Can of engine oil
Can of transmission oil
Spare flashlight batteries
Spare globes for cabin, navigation, and other lights

These lists are by no means exhaustive, for the tool and spares inventories vary a great deal depending on the complexity and size of the charter yacht. However, most charterers assume that you need enough tools and spares to make routine adjustments, and to get yourself to port without outside help. No one expects you to undertake major repairs.

At check-out time, be sure to inventory the contents of the spares and tool kits, so that you can ask for any essential missing items.

Fuel and Fuel Consumption

The charter company will send you out with a full tank of diesel, so it behooves you to know something of the range of the yacht under power. To calculate this, you need the following information:

- The **fuel capacity of the tank**. This averages about 90 gallons on large yachts.
- The **fuel consumption** of the engine at full speed and at cruising speed.
- The **speed of the yacht** through the water at full and cruising speed.

The following diagram shows you how to calculate range:

$$S_{peed} \times C_{onsumption} = D_{istance} \; P_{er} \; G_{allon}$$
$$\text{(in one hour)}$$

$$DPG \times Ca_{pacity} = R_{ange}$$

Figure 3-14 *(1). Check on board manuals for boat's cruising speed and engine fuel consumption. Convert consumption to a one hour value. Example ... 1 gallon / 20 min. = 3 gallons / hour. (2). Multiply speed by consumption to get D.P.G. (3). Find the yacht's fuel capacity. (4). Multiply D.P.G. by capacity to get range. (5). A realistic range is 7/8 of this value. Engines run a higher risk of malfunctioning where fuel levels dip below 1/8 tank.*

This calculation will allow you to estimate whether refueling will be necessary during a long passage, and also to keep track of fuel consumption during a long charter.

The following factors can affect the range of your yacht under power:

- **Speed of the yacht.** The faster you power, the more fuel you use. Diesel consumption can rise fast once you exceed cruising speed.

- **Wind conditions.** A following wind can increase your range (and I hope you are sailing under this condition). A strong head wind can slow you down a great deal.

- **Whether you are motor sailing or not**. A well trimmed sail can give you a knot or more in favorable conditions (see Motor Sailing).

- **Sea and swell conditions**. Bumpy conditions on the bow can make a radical difference to your progress. A violent head sea can slow you to a virtual standstill.

- **The weight of the vessel,** especially the load carried aboard. Heavier laden yachts are more easily slowed by adverse wind or sea conditions than lighter craft.

- **Bottom condition**: a dirty hull slows you down.

This completes the Ashore portion of Section 3, except for the Review Questions.

REVIEW QUESTIONS

1. List FOUR items you should check daily on your engine:

   1. _____
   2. _____
   3. _____
   4. _____

2. List SIX important spare parts that should be aboard your charter yacht:

   1. _____
   2. _____
   3. _____
   4. _____
   5. _____
   6. _____

3. If your engine fails to turn over at starting time, do you check:

   a. The fuel filters
   b. The water intake
   c. The battery terminals

4. Describe how you bleed a diesel fuel system (four lines):

   _____
   _____
   _____
   _____

AFLOAT SKILLS

Section 3's time afloat is spent entirely under power. There will be plenty of time to sail later, so let us concentrate on learning how to handle the boat with the engine under a wide variety of circumstances.

We will, however, need the mainsail, so you should take off the main cover at the slip before starting out. Do not set the sail or undo the ties from the boom. It will be some time before we use it.

For the purposes of this lesson, we assume that you are under way and powered into open water, applying the principles of maneuvering under power that we learned earlier. Now that we are clear of other traffic and the shore, we can start on today's specific skills.

Stopping the Boat at a Fixed Marker

There are many occasions when you may have to stop your vessel at a mooring buoy or some other stationary object in the water. You may have anchored your dinghy somewhere while you take off on a short sail, or need to come bow to a pier to pick up a crew member.

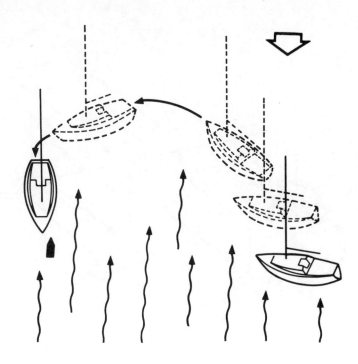

Figure 3-15b *Approaching a mooring where the wind and current oppose one another.*

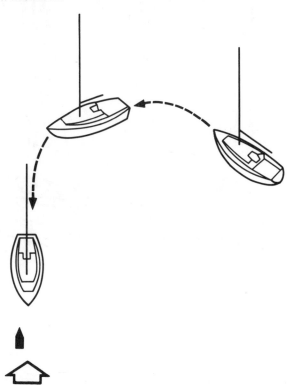

Figure 3-15a *One method of reaching a marker from down-wind is to approach close hauled and come head-to-wind about two boat lengths below the mark. Your momentum should carry you to the mark once the drifting distance has been established.*

Choose a suitable marker, or even lay a special one for the purpose. Now it is time to begin. You are powering along at cruising speed when the moment to come up to the marker arrives. Whatever the weather conditions, always:

1. **Reduce engine speed** to idle with the gear lever in forward while you assess the situation. While the boat slows down, note:

   - The wind direction and strength
   - The current and tidal streams, if any.

Plan your approach with these factors in mind. Here are the general principles you should follow:

   a. **Approach the marker from downwind** and down-current if possible, so that they apply brakes, as it were, to your forward movement.

   b. If wind and current/tide are opposite one another, **approach against the strongest** of the two.

There are, of course, variations on these two situations, but as a matter of general principle, you approach **against** the stronger force, overcoming the other with boat speed and steering.

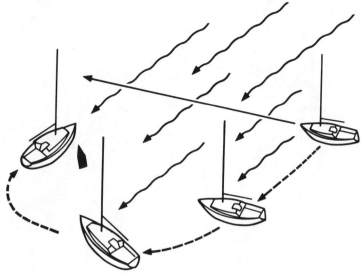

Figure 3-15c *With wind and current abeam, helmsman steers upwind of the marker and eventually lands at the desired destination.*

Casting off a Mooring

Casting off a mooring or buoy seems like simplicity itself, but can be tricky, especially in strong winds and currents. Here is a simple procedure:

1. **Start engine.** Station a crew member at the bow ready to cast off.

2. Assess relative strengths of wind and current, and check positions of nearby vessels.

3. **Cast off,** steering the bow to port or starboard with the wheel, depending on space available and direction of wind and current. This sheer enables the mooring line to drop clear of the keel and propellor.
   The crew member throws the mooring WELL CLEAR of the bow, making sure the line goes into the water without snagging the lifelines or bow pulpit.

4. Once clear, **apply power** and steer clear of other vessels to open water.

2. **Delegate a crew member** to take the boathook to the bow ready to catch the marker. Another crew member is assigned amidships to relay directions and keep a lookout.

The essence of picking up a marker is to control your speed up to the buoy and to judge the moment to go into neutral as exactly as possible. You should use as little stern way as possible as you approach. Picking up a marker like this requires very nice judgement and practice. Try it several times, so that you get the hang of the way in which the vessel carries her way. ASA's charter standard calls for being within four feet of the marker. You should aim to be right on the button every time, however.

The diagrams labeled figures 3-15 A,B,C,D show you the procedures to follow in:
   - wind heading you conditions,
   - wind and current flowing in opposite directions,
   - wind and/or current from astern,
   - wind and/or current from quarter or beam.

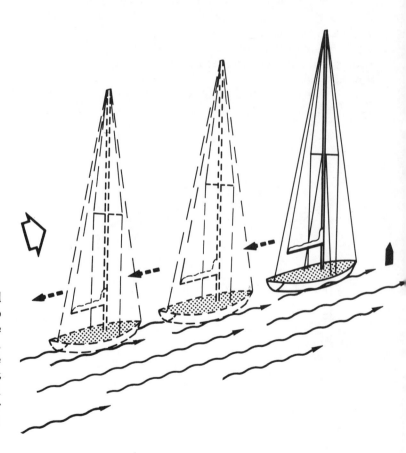

Figure 3-15d *When wind and current both come from astern, reverse must be used to ease the vessel down to the marker. This method would only be useful for a mooring pickup where there is very little room to maneuver down-wind of the mooring.*

Motor Sailing

Motor sailing is a commonplace way of passage making when on charter, especially when you experience headwinds and want to make port before darkness falls. Your time on the water is precious, so you motor sail to save time, too.

Many charterers blindly motor to windward with their sails flapping, not only making slower progress but ruining the sails as well. You should learn to motor sail properly, if nothing else so that you can make added speed on uncomfortable days.

Set the mainsail, while a hand steers the boat slowly head-to-wind.

Once the main is hoisted and trimmed hard-in, sail to windward on the port or starboard tack.

1. **Steer the boat closehauled** with the engine idling. The yacht will move gently along, heeling slightly to the puffs. Progress will be slow, except in a relatively high performance yacht.

2. **Now increase power** to cruising speed. Speed through the water increases. Monitor the knotmeter, and check the speed before and after applying power.

3. **Keep on the same tack** for five minutes, checking how close to the wind you can sail with the main filling. It will probably be around 30 to 35 degrees.

4. **Come about** onto the other tack, and do the same for five minutes.

ALWAYS MOTOR SAIL WITH THE SAIL(S) FILLING. DO NOT ALLOW THEM TO LUFF.

Motor sailing with the main alone steadies the ship in bumpy water, and enables you to maintain a steady course. If the sails are luffing, you lose the advantage of having them set at all.

Now unroll the jib, and try motor sailing to windward on both tacks with both sails filling. Check the speed of the boat under sail alone, then use the throttle to bring her up to normal cruising speed under power. Chances are you will save fuel by being able to throttle back, allowing the sails to do part of the work.

Motor sailing under both main and jib is highly effective in light airs, when you have to make your way to windward on a schedule.

Sometimes you see people motoring or motor-sailing on passage with the wind behind them or on the beam, when there is more than enough breeze for sails alone. They are wasting gas and exhibiting poor seamanship. Please, dear reader, do not be one of them...

Once you are used to the feel of motor-sailing, motor sail to a position several miles offshore, then lower the sails. Follow the procedures you learned earlier in the course. You are several miles away from harbor. There is a reason for this. It is time for some coastal navigation.

Figure 3-16

Reading a Chart

Approaching any unknown port means using both a chart and local sailing directions to identify both the general location of the harbor and the details of the entrance itself.

Please note that the techniques we are about to teach you are extremely basic, and are generally not enough in themselves to allow you to navigate safely into a strange harbor. They do, however, represent a beginning.

One way to carry out this exercise is to stop the yacht. With the boat stationary, and the general approach chart in front of you, identify the following:

- Major geographical features like headlands, hills, or estuaries that mark the general location of the harbor.
- Conspicuous, light colored buildings or lighthouses, water towers, or radio towers that lie directly behind the harbor entrance.
- Offlying navigation buoys or other markers that indicate precise lines of approach.

Having identified these in real life, now identify them on the chart, with the chart oriented along the ship's head, which should be pointing toward land.

Fixing Your Position

We are going to plot a course to the harbor entrance. However, you must first fix your position on the chart. For this exercise, bring out a HAND BEARING COMPASS, NAVIGATIONAL DIVIDERS, a pencil and eraser, and a pair of PARALLEL RULERS or equivalent, as well as the actual chart for the area — so you can plot your position directly onto it.

Figure 3-18 *Hand bearing compass in use.*

The HAND BEARING COMPASS (a portable compass used for fixing the position of the ship) takes many forms. The most common designs are either compasses with a special sight set on a short handle,

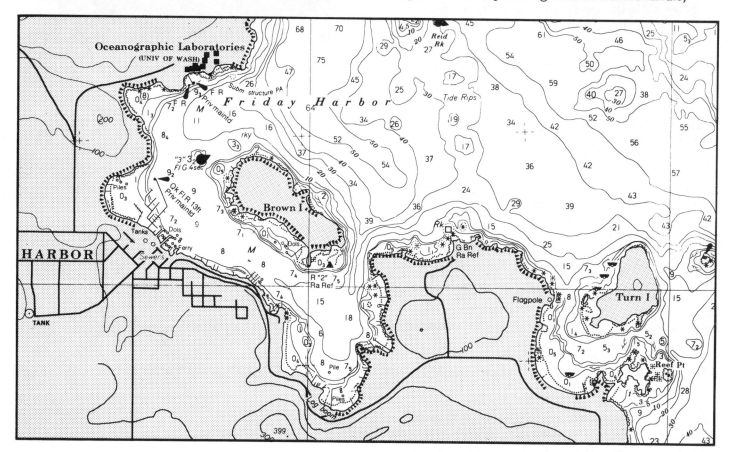

Figure 3-17 *A typical small craft harbor. Notice the chart symbols on the water as well as on the land.*

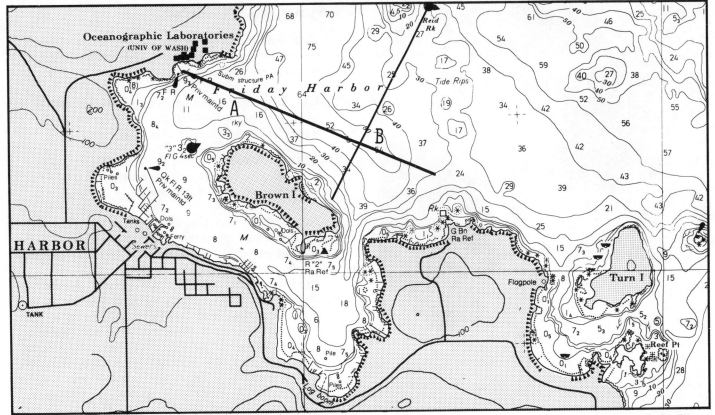

Figure 3-19 *(A) A Line of Position (LOP). (B) When two LOP's intersect, the point at which they touch is called a Fix.*

or, even better, small instruments that you hold close to your eye. Whichever design is aboard, the principle is the same.

Hold the compass up to your eye. If necessary adjust the sight, so that the LUBBER LINE, in this case the sighting line, is clearly visible, with a turning set of compass headings immediately under it. These numbers show the compass head in degrees magnetic. Now take a bearing on one of the conspicuous landmarks you identified earlier (a large building marked on the chart is ideal).

1. **Brace yourself against the ship's movement,** well away from the engine and main compass, which could affect compass reading.
2. **Identify object** for bearing.
3. **Train the compass sighting line** on the object, with the instrument up to your eye.
4. **Allow time** for the compass reading to steady. When it is stationary, take the bearing at the point where the line bisects the numbered circle.
5. **Call out the reading,** so that someone writes it down.

You now have a reading, a line of sight from your (unknown) position to an identifiable landmark. When plotted on the chart, this is known as a LINE OF POSITION. (We will plot your reading in a moment)

Obviously, a single line on the chart does not give you a position, so we need at least one more intersecting bearing to fix our position. You establish the ship's position by two or more compass bearings on landmarks of known position.

To take your FIX, you must obtain at least one more BEARING, preferably two, using landmarks

Figure 3-20 *A navigator transfers the information from the hand bearing compass on deck to the chart.*

Figure 3-21 *Once we have determined our position, we can now proceed to our destination.*

that are at wide angles to one another. This will give you a more accurate fix.

Now take these bearings with the yacht still stationary.

With the bearings safely written down, we can now plot the fix on the chart.

1. **Lay out the chart** on the chart table.

2. **Identify the three landmarks** on the chart.

3. **Take each bearing in turn, and lay it out across the compass rose** on the chart nearest to your harbor. USE THE MAGNETIC COMPASS ROSE FOR THIS PURPOSE.

4. Using the parallel rulers, **transfer the bearing to the landmark,** each bearing in turn, drawing light lines on the chart through the landmarks out to sea.

5. The three bearing lines intersect. You are at the point where they cross.

It may be that there is a small triangle of ocean between the three lines. This is known as the "cocked hat," and marks your position. With coastal bearings, this is usually of small size, and therefore insignificant.

Laying off a Course

Now that we know where we are, we can lay off a course to the harbor entrance, and establish the distance and estimated time of arrival.

1. **Lay the parallel rulers** from your fixed position to the harbor entrance on the chart. Draw a light pencil line between the two points.

2. **Transfer the line** to the MAGNETIC circle of the compass rose and read off the course. This is your course to steer to the harbor.

Now set the yacht on this course using the ship's compass. As you approach the entrance, pick up the major landmarks on the chart and get out the large scale plan.

At this point, identify the major landmarks leading to the harbor entrance and the buoys and other markers that lead you to the fairway into port. To help you in this exercise, the accompanying illustration shows you some of the major chart symbols that you will encounter in such exercises. These are symbols that you will use again and again

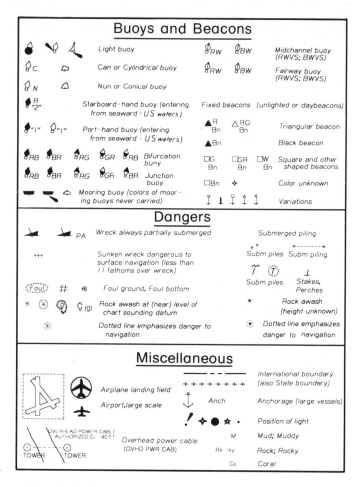

Figure 3-22 *Some common chart symbols and their meanings.*

when you charter in different areas, so it is worth memorizing the major ones.

We will practice pilotage in Section 4, when we take a passage to another port.

PLEASE NOTE THAT WE HAVE ASSUMED THAT THERE IS NO TIDE OR CURRENT TO DISTURB YOUR COURSE SETTINGS FOR THE PURPOSE OF THESE EXERCISES.

Once you are safely in port, find an uncongested dock where you can learn how to secure your yacht stern-to a quay, a way of securing alongside that is commonplace in many charter areas.

Securing Bow- or Stern-To

This method of securing a yacht is used in congested harbors where numerous vessels need to use the same quay space. You will practice this maneuver in an area where there is plenty of room to turn, but be aware that in many places you will have much less margin for error.

The diagrams and commentaries that follow show you how to:
- secure bow-to a quay with the anchor over the stern,
- secure stern-to a quay with the anchor over the bow.

These exercises require considerable practice and skill. However, they will go much more smoothly if you always:
1. **Delegate crew members** to specific tasks well ahead of time. Specifically, have bow or stern lines coiled and ready to use, with people ready to take them ashore.
2. **Have some of the anchor rode flaked on deck,** and anchor ready to let go immediately.
3. **Have the dinghy alongside**, if available, ready to take lines ashore.
4. **Hands with fenders** should be ready to place them wherever they are needed at short notice.

Stern-to is a trickier exercise, but has the advantage of convenience, in that you can lay a gang plank ashore from the aft deck. However, you will have less privacy, and there is always a danger that your rudder will ground on an underwater obstruction that is invisible until you hit it.

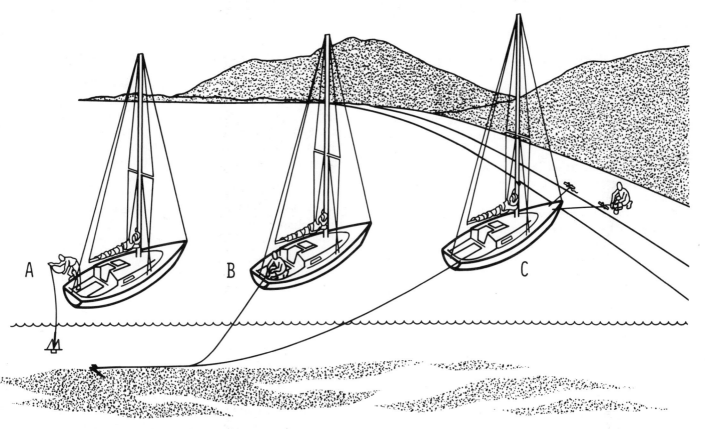

Figure 3-23a *(A) Anchor is lowered over the stern. (B) Crew snubs anchor. (C) Proper scope is laid out and bow gets attached to the seawall or quay.*

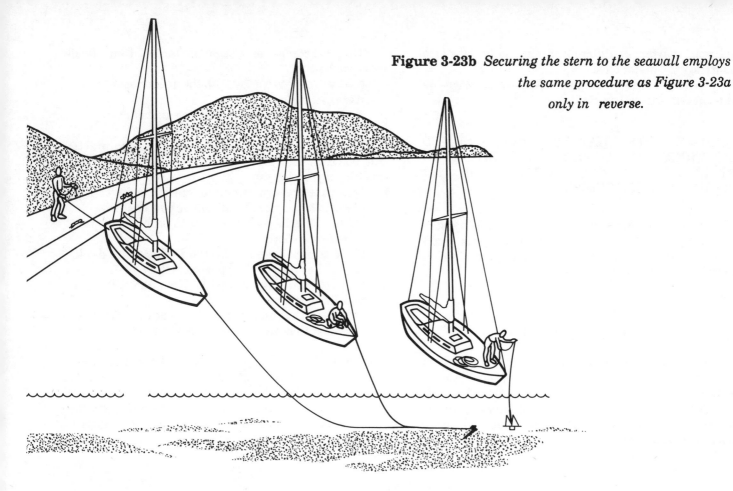

Figure 3-23b *Securing the stern to the seawall employs the same procedure as Figure 3-23a only in reverse.*

Laying an Anchor to Windward

Once you have completed these exercises, secure alongside a dock where the wind is blowing onto the quay. If there is any sea running, the yacht will grind against her fenders. Are there ways in which you can control the grinding?

One common solution is to lay an anchor to windward to keep you off the dock. There are two ways of doing this.

Many people take the stern anchor and lay it out some distance with the dinghy, then haul the line taut from the yacht to ease her away from the quay. This works fine provided the wind is not blowing too strongly, and you have a good snub.

The diagram shows you a much easier way to achieve the same goal. Before starting the maneuver, however, have fenders rigged on the leeward side, bow and stern lines, as well as spring lines ready for use, and the crew delegated to specific tasks. The bow anchor should be ready for immediate use. Once these preparations are made, take care to assess wind and current direction, as you will have no chance to change your mind once the maneuver is under way.

To cast off, the anchor line is slacked off and brought to the bow, then used to haul the bow offshore, as fenders are used to cushion the stern.

Alternatively, you can use a spring line to lever the yacht off the wall.

Securing Alongside a Wall when There is a Large Tidal Range

Most charter areas do not boast of very large tidal ranges, but you should be aware of what to do if there is a considerable tidal range and you want to secure alongside a fixed dock. This could be ten feet out of the water and low tide, and only three at high water. Floating marinas rise and fall with the tide, with gangways on rollers, so you do not have to adjust your ropes. But a tidal harbor presents quite different problems.

Firstly, you will have to calculate if there is sufficient depth of water for your yacht at low tide (see illustration). Secondly, you will have to allow for rising and falling water levels at your berth.

The diagram shows you how to secure safely alongside in a tidal harbor, and how to adjust your lines:

Once you have learned how to use an anchor at the dock, Section 3 is complete.

Section 4 follows, a lesson about passage-making that takes you on a short passage to an anchorage and back. It is, perhaps, a good thing to combine Sections 4 and 5 in a two-day cruise so that you can experience an overnight trip afloat, one of the great joys of chartering.

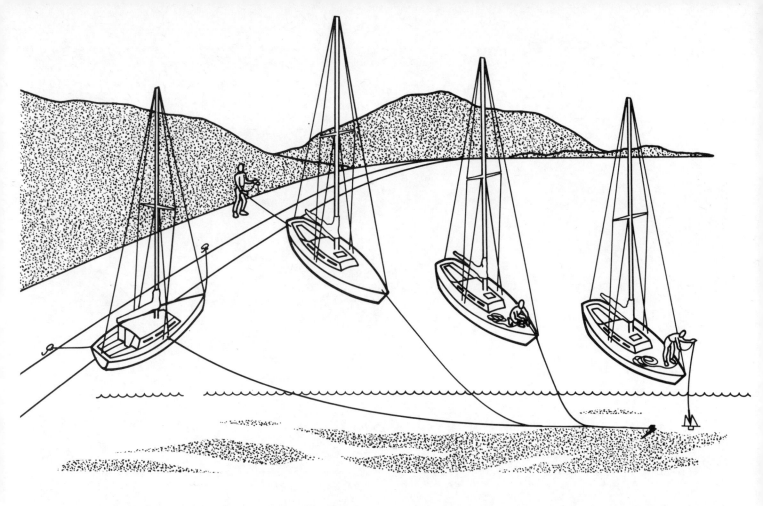

Figure 3-24 *The anchor rode holds the boat off the seawall while resting beam-to the wall. Anchor is set similarly to Figure 23b but one step is added.*

Figure 3-25 *In an area where the tide falls enough to expose the bottom, a line running from a shroud to the shore ensures that the boat leans with its deck toward higher ground. Padding the hull will reduce the chances of damage. This situation should be avoided if at all possible.*

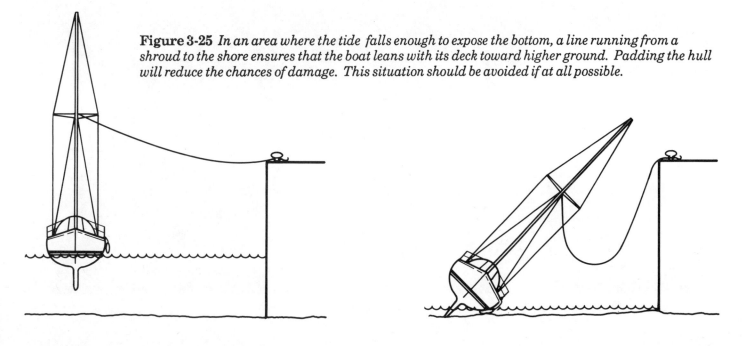

Figure 4-1

SECTION 4
PASSAGE MAKING

ASHORE KNOWLEDGE

Section 4 is where we put all the knowledge of yacht handling you have acquired together. This, and **Section 5,** can be taken together, as part of the 48-hour cruise that you carry out as your final qualifier for the Bareboating Certification. **Section 4** takes you on a passage from home port to an anchorage some distance away (the mileage will vary according to the location where you are taking the course), covers the planning of such a passage, and locating, entering, and anchoring in the anchorage at the other end. **Section 5** carries on and deals with living aboard.

The **Ashore Knowledge** part of **Section 4** covers planning your passage. This time you spend longer afloat actually making the passage.

Planning the Passage

All passages begin with planning before you get under way, checking the weather forecast, laying out courses, and researching alternative anchorages.

Planning your passage can be divided into three sections:
- Preparing the yacht herself,
- Planning the navigation,
- Checking the weather conditions.
- Preparing the crew and passengers' personal gear.

Preparing the Yacht

We have covered some of the ground before, but here is a checklist of the major items you should check before taking off on passage, or on a charter cruise for that matter:
- All **mechanical and electrical systems,** also electronics, in proper working order,
- **Sails and running gear** rigged, ready to set, including reefing lines,
- **Ground tackle** properly secured and ready for instant use,
- All **emergency gear** is aboard, in proper working order, and the crew instructed in its location and use,
- **Fuel, water, and cooking fuel tanks full.**
- All **provisions are aboard,** sufficient for duration of the trip, and stowed properly.
- **Navigational equipment** is in order and large and small scale charts are aboard. Coast pilots covering the area are carried.
- **Head and stove** are functioning properly, and crew have been instructed in use of same.
- **Bilges** have been pumped out.
- All **personal baggage** is stowed away, so that it will not roll around in rough water.

In addition, you should follow the check list for leaving harbor you learned in **Section 1.**

Figure 4-2

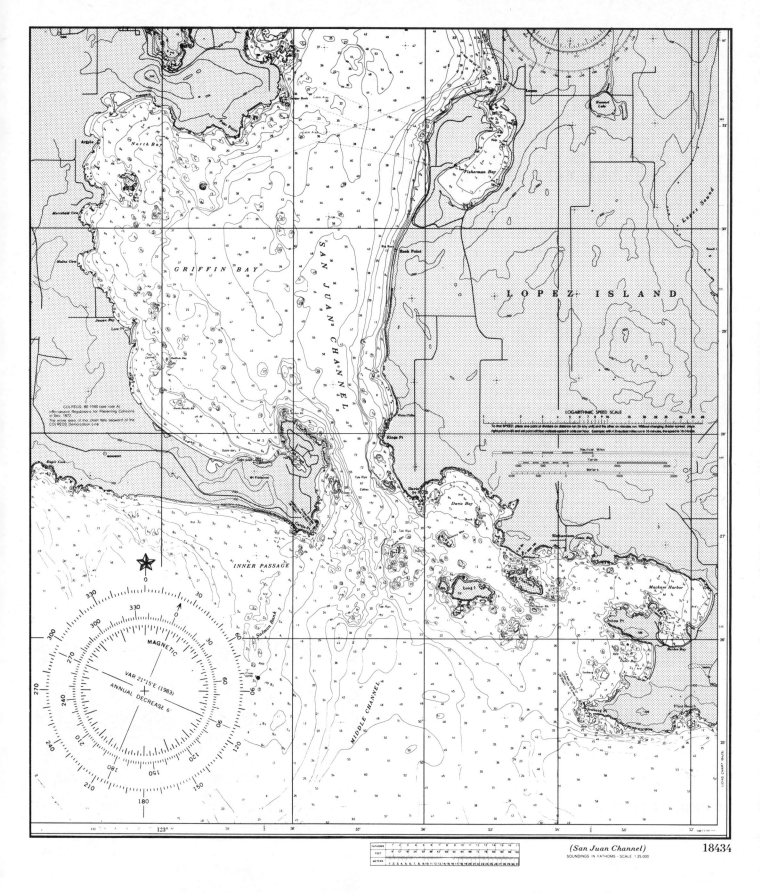

Figure 4-3 *Every bit of information on a nautical chart is important. Our Afloat Skills voyage will bring us through the San Juan Channel. Begin to notice chart characteristics.*

The essence of preparing the vessel is to be prepared for sudden rough weather, and to ensure that all the gear you need is aboard. IT IS ESPECIALLY IMPORTANT TO HAVE THE CORRECT CHARTS, COAST PILOTS AND HARBOR PLANS ABOARD, as these are critical information in the event of diversion to another anchorage in rough weather.

Navigational Preparation

Correct preparation means having:

• The courses to steer laid out in advance on the chart.
• As part of this process, you should calculate:
 - Time of departure
 - State of the tide at moment of departure
 - Estimated time of passage under prevailing weather conditions.
 - State of the tide at estimated time of arrival.
 - Weather forecast for the next 24 hours, and some long range projections as well.
• Detailed notes on the destination port or anchorage kept close to the plan or chart, distilled from the sailing directions, so you can make decisions as to where to anchor and so on without constantly referring to the book and chart.
• Information on alternative anchorages or ports close to hand, so that you can divert to another location at short notice if weather, congestion, or other unforeseeable circumstances so dictate.

The planning process can be seen as a sequence of tasks:

1. Take out the chart covering the area of your passage and **lay off the magnetic course** between your home port and your destination. This may involve a single course, or a series of courses from, say, a certain distance off one headland to the next until you reach your destination.
2. In areas where tide is a significant factor, **use the tide tables to check times of high and low tide,** and the tidal current chart to calculate direction and velocity of tidal streams during your passage. Then add the necessary allowances for these to your courses. (Readers interested in how to do this should consult ASA's Coastal Navigation course: we assume that there are no tides for purposes of the chartering course). Perhaps consult local sailors for tide and current information.
3. **Estimate your time of arrival** using your estimated average speed, as you learned in **Section 3.** If necessary, allow for adverse tides in making your calculation.

4. Examine the chart carefully and **note all major landmarks** that you may see on passage, those that will allow you to take fixes and establish your position. These can include **lighthouses, headlands, large structures ashore like power plants, conspicuous rocks,** and so on. **Read the sailing directions** for the coastline, looking out for warnings of special dangers. For instance, they may warn that "outlying rocks and reefs extend offshore for at least a mile at this vicinity. You should keep at least twice this distance offshore to avoid inshore setting currents." You will have to adjust your course on the chart accordingly.
5. Read up on the sailing directions for your destination contained in the local cruising guide, if such a volume exists. Study them in conjunction with the chart.

San Juan Channel, the middle one of three principal channels leading from the Strait of Juan de Fuca to the Strait of Georgia, separates San Juan Island from the islands E. It is 13 miles long from its S end to its junction with President Channel at the N end. San Juan Channel is deep throughout and, except near its S entrance, has few off-lying dangers.
Currents.–In the S end of San Juan Channel, between Goose Island and Deadman Island, the average current velocity is 2.6 knots on the flood and ebb, however, maximum flood currents of 5 knots or more cause severe rips and eddies. Daily current predictions for this location may be obtained from the Tidal Current Tables.
Cattle Point, marked by a light and a seasonal fog signal, is the SE extremity of San Juan Island and forms the W point at the S entrance to San Juan Channel. Cattle were once loaded here for shipment to and from Victoria.
Salmon Bank, S of Cattle Point and on the W side of **Middle Channel,** is an extensive shoal covered 1½ to 3 fathoms; it is marked by a lighted gong buoy. Kelp grows on the rocks. **Whale Rocks,** two dark rocks about 5 feet high, are on the E side of Middle Channel 0.6 mile W of Long Island. There are 2¼-fathom spots nearby.

Figure 4-4 *A section from* <u>Coast Pilot</u> *describes our cruising area.*

Study the place from three perspectives:
Approach: What landmarks ashore enable you to identify the place? Are there buoys, conspicuous headlands, or lighthouses that lead you in? Do they display distinctive colors, like, for example, "a rose-colored cliff face marks the eastern side of the entrance"?
Are there offlying dangers that hinder your approach, deep water reefs or an approach channel to be identified?

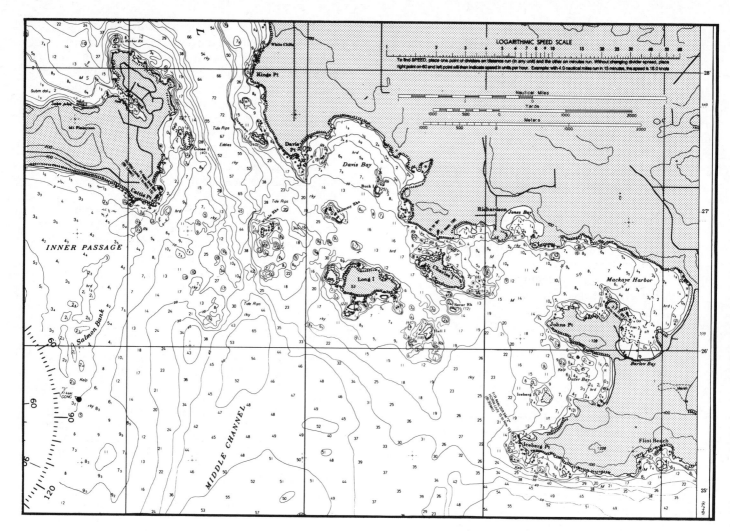

Figure 4-5 *A closer view of navigation area.*

Entrance: Once the approach is identified, what about the entrance itself? Is there buoyage that marks a channel into the anchorage or port? How wide is it? Is there sufficient depth for our draft? Are there leading marks that lead you into the channel along a set line? Can the channel be negotiated at night? Be sure that you have noted the salient features of the entrance before you set out, so you do not have to spend your time in a last minute flurry of reading.

Berths: Where are the best places to anchor? Are there special docks for visiting yachts? What about adequate swinging room? Does one have to lay two anchors? Is there adequate shelter from strong winds? What about congestion?

It should be emphasized that this is all theoretical planning at this point. Weather conditions may change, you may suffer a mechanical breakdown, or the anchorage may be too crowded when you arrive. The secret of planning is to keep your plans flexible, so you can change anchorages or shorten a voyage at short notice.

6. Develop information on alternative anchorages and ports both short of, and beyond, your destination. For example, if the wind pipes up, you may want to divert into a nearby port for shelter. Your destination may be crammed with week-ending yachts. But just round the corner lies a comfortable cove that is nearly empty. Since you know there is sufficient depth there, you can divert at very short notice.

The secret of successful chartering is careful passage planning.

Checking the weather

You can do most of your planning without considering weather conditions, as you track the weather forecasts for a few days before your departure. Indeed, you should keep an ear open for the weather every four hours during your charter, especially in areas where weather can be unpredictable, or if you are chartering in the Caribbean, the Gulf of Mexico, or on the East Coast during hurricane season.

Weather forecasts can be obtained in a number of ways:

• By **telephoning the local weather service**. If this is possible, you will normally find the number in sailing directions or the charter company will give it to you. This type of forecast is normally fairly comprehensive, but in some busy places will consist of a recorded message. If you are lucky enough to get a real forecaster, he or she may give you invaluable, informal assessments of the future outlook that are more useful than any number of recorded forecasts.

• By **listening to commercial radio stations** or **watching TV new**s broadcasts. Unfortunately, these are usually sketchy at best and oriented toward people living ashore. They rarely mention wind directions or the outlook for more than 6 hours, when you need something with a longer duration. Even marine forecasts, if broadcast at all, are very curtailed.

The exceptions are overseas. European radio stations broadcast extended marine forecasts that predict wind direction, sea conditions, and visibility, as well as giving a general synopsis of air mass conditions over a large area. Sailing directions or the charter company will tell you what time these are broadcast, and what wave lengths are used.

• **Recorded official forecasts** broadcast on VHF radio channel W-1 or W-2, which you can pick up on your VHF. This is the most common source of weather information in the US. The forecasts are updated every six to twelve hours. They give you a rapid general synopsis, which enables you to track the approach of low pressure disturbances, a forecast for surrounding sea and coastal areas, and a general outlook beyond the next few hours.

Unless the weather is very settled, you should plan on tracking the weather forecasts over several days before your charter begins, so that you have an impression of how the weather is moving across your area. This will enable you to judge, say, the intervals between "lows," or the timing of a weakening high pressure area. Such timings can be invaluable when making short passages in unfavorable weather, so you can maximize the lulls between weather systems.

By tracking forecasts over several days, you can get an excellent idea of prevailing weather, and shape your charter cruise accordingly. Here are some phenomena that you should take into account when planning your passage:

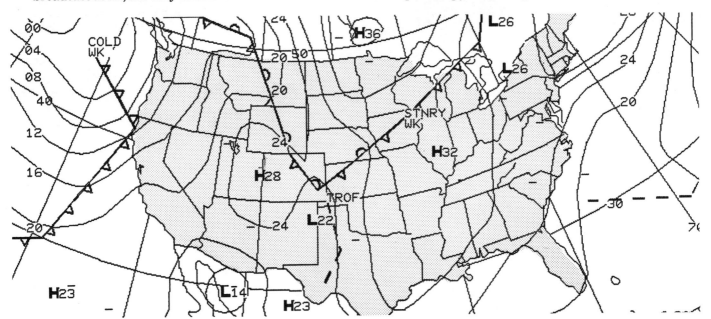

Figure 4-6 *A synoptic weather chart.*

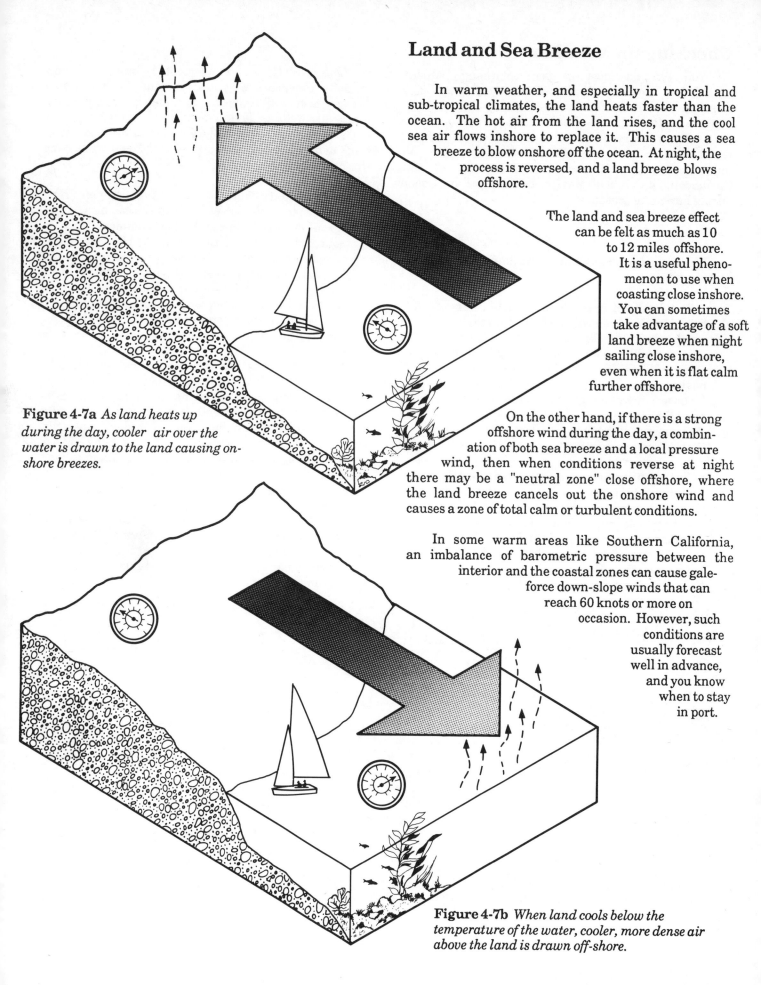

Land and Sea Breeze

In warm weather, and especially in tropical and sub-tropical climates, the land heats faster than the ocean. The hot air from the land rises, and the cool sea air flows inshore to replace it. This causes a sea breeze to blow onshore off the ocean. At night, the process is reversed, and a land breeze blows offshore.

The land and sea breeze effect can be felt as much as 10 to 12 miles offshore. It is a useful phenomenon to use when coasting close inshore. You can sometimes take advantage of a soft land breeze when night sailing close inshore, even when it is flat calm further offshore.

On the other hand, if there is a strong offshore wind during the day, a combination of both sea breeze and a local pressure wind, then when conditions reverse at night there may be a "neutral zone" close offshore, where the land breeze cancels out the onshore wind and causes a zone of total calm or turbulent conditions.

In some warm areas like Southern California, an imbalance of barometric pressure between the interior and the coastal zones can cause gale-force down-slope winds that can reach 60 knots or more on occasion. However, such conditions are usually forecast well in advance, and you know when to stay in port.

Figure 4-7a *As land heats up during the day, cooler air over the water is drawn to the land causing on-shore breezes.*

Figure 4-7b *When land cools below the temperature of the water, cooler, more dense air above the land is drawn off-shore.*

Fog

Foggy conditions can be as dangerous as gale-force winds and seas, especially when you are crossing shipping lanes. You must exercise special care in passage planning when fog is forecast.

Fog is caused by abrupt temperature changes, such as those that occur when warm air comes into contact with cold air. Minute water drops condense into fog, just like they do when a kettle boils. FOG IS PARTICULARLY HAZARDOUS BECAUSE IT CAN FORM AT A MOMENT'S NOTICE, especially in calm conditions. You may have set off on passage on a beautiful day, only to become enveloped in dense fog, with only a few yards of visibility. You can become disoriented, sounds are distorted, and the effect is both dangerous and eerie.

As air temperature decreases, so relative humidity increases, until saturation takes place and any further cooling results in condensation of some of the moisture. The temperature at which this occurs is called the DEW POINT. Dew or frost now form on the ground. Fog is formed of millions of visible droplets formed by condensation of water vapor in the air, in effect a cloud that is in contact with the surface of the earth. When the air temperature and dew point coincide, fog occurs.

There are two types of fog which can affect cruise planning:

RADIATION FOG: forms over low-lying land on calm nights, forming a temperature inversion when the land cools the air immediately above the surface. So the temperature rises with altitude, with a surface fog where the air has cooled to its dew point.

Figure 4-8 *Photo: Leslie Newhart*

This type of fog is common in the early mornings and often vanishes when the sun warms up the land. Southern California sailors experience this phenomenon during the summer months.

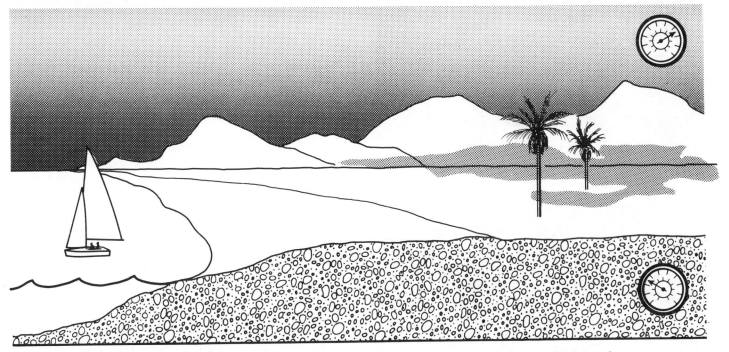

Figure 4-9a *The lowest lying areas will be coolest causing fog to form only near the ground.*

ADVECTION FOG: forms when warm, moist air blows over a colder surface and is cooled below its dew point. This type of sea fog can be very dense and persist over considerable periods of time. Sailors sometimes call this "pea soup fog."

Figure 4-9b

HAZE AND SMOG (a mixture of haze and smoke) are commonplace off our industrialized coasts. These can restrict your ability to spot landmarks from offshore. Check the visibility locally as you leave port so that you can adjust your thinking about landmarks at the other end accordingly.

Figure 4-10 *L.A. smog*

Fortunately, most charter companies operate in areas where the weather conditions are relatively predictable. With even reasonable luck, you should be able to enjoy fine weather conditions throughout your cruise. Here, however, are some hints on navigating in foggy conditions:

• Sound the fog signals required under COLREGS and hoist your Radar Reflector.

• Set a course that takes you out of shipping lanes and clear of any potential navigational dangers. If in shallow water and in no immediate danger, anchor until the fog lifts.

• Turn on navigation lights. They can often be seen at a greater distance than the hull or rigging.

• If there is the slightest risk of encountering other vessels or running aground, reduce speed to allow for poor visibility.

• If in doubt, stop the ship, turn off the engine, and listen. Noise carries in fog, even if it can be deceiving. Use your depth meter to navigate inshore clear of shipping lanes.

• If in harbor contemplating a passage, stay in port until the fog lifts.

• As visibility deteriorates, update your DEAD RECKONING POSITION (the position of the vessel calculated on the basis of compass course steered, speed of yacht, and allowances for tide and current, a position established WITHOUT fixing the ship with landmarks, radio beacons, or other means) and try to fix the ship's position from nearby landmarks. This provides a basis for setting an accurate course when the fog settles in. Update your DR as frequently as you can, and set a course out of shipping lanes.

• Keep silence aboard, and listen carefully for fog signals from other vessels. It is a good idea to station a lookout in the bow, especially when operating in shipping lanes or close to shallows or land.

Figure 4-11 *A keen lookout reduces the danger of navigation in the fog.*

Travel and Ship's Documents

Even in home waters, your charter yacht should carry some identification, usually her Federal or State registration papers. Check that these are aboard before you leave.

Some charter areas, like the Grenadines or English Channel, require that you cross international borders. For such crossings you will need:

- The vessel's State or Federal registration documents.
- Passports for each member of the crew. Some countries will admit you on the basis of a driver's license or some other such identification, but do not count on it. CHECK ALL POSSIBLE CUSTOMS AND IMMIGRATIONS REGULATIONS IN ADVANCE. It may be too late to comply with the correct documents once you arrive.
- Some countries require a cruising permit or evidence of insurance coverage. The former is obtained at the port of entry, the other is provided by the charter company.

When leaving for another country, you are usually required to clear customs and immigration upon departure and to enter your destination country at a Port of Entry, a place where customs and immigration facilities are established, normally a larger port. You cannot travel elsewhere without having gone through entry procedures. You must also go through customs and immigration upon your return to your home country. These can often be fulfilled by using a toll-free telephone number.

Your charter company will provide you with information on procedures if you plan to visit another country during your charter.

Customs Ports of Entry and Stations 15
Vessels may be entered and cleared at any port of entry or customs station, but at the latter only with advance authorization from the Customs Service district director.

Pacific Region 20
San Diego District:
Port of Entry: San Diego.
Los Angeles District:
Ports of Entry: Los Angeles-Long Beach, Port San Luis. 25

Customs Station: Port Hueneme.
San Francisco District:
Ports of Entry: San Francisco-Oakland, Eureka.
Customs Station: Monterey.
Columbia-Snake (at Portland) District: 30
Ports of Entry: Astoria, Coos Bay, Longview, Newport.

Seattle District:
Ports of Entry: Aberdeen, Blaine, Point Roberts, Puget Sound (includes Anacortes, Bellingham, Everett, Friday Harbor, Neah Bay, Olympia, Port Angeles, Port Townsend, and Tacoma). 35

Honolulu District:
Ports of Entry: Hilo, Honolulu, Kahului, Nawiliwili-Port Allen. 40

Figure 4-12 *Customs information from Coast Pilot.*

Tides and Tidal Range

In some parts of the world, the direction of tidal streams dictate the times at which you head out of port, start passages, and end them. Why fight the tides, when a few hours later they will carry you to your chosen destination, with extra speed as a bonus? You can pay less heed to the tides in areas with smaller **tidal ranges** (the difference in height between extreme high and extreme low tide), but you will still have to take account of them when anchoring in shallow water. This means you must be able to calculate the tidal range at any moment during the tidal cycle. It is no joke to anchor in comfort on a falling tide, only to find yourself hard aground and on your ear in the small hours because you miscalculated the depth at low water.

The best analogy is the water running out of a sink when the plug is removed. How much water do you need under your keel to remain afloat at low water? To calculate this figure you need:

- **A set of tide tables** for your cruising area. These will give you:

  - The times of high and low water,
  - The range of the tide on a given date. Note that this varies dramatically between spring and neap tides, according to the phases of the moon.
  - The tidal differences between your destination and the "Standard Ports", the major ports where tidal data are recorded.

These tables will give you time and height differences.

- **The draft of your yacht.** If you are uncertain of this, a figure of six feet is a pretty reliable estimate for a 40-footer.
- **The time** at which you expect to anchor.
- **The charted depth** at the spot where you want to anchor. This will be depth relative to chart datum (a baseline used on charts which coincides with lowest low water).

Here is the procedure for calculating how much water there will be under your keel at low tide:

- **Find the day's tidal range.** (Subtract the height of the day's low tide from the reading for high tide to get range).
- **Find the time of high and low water** for the day, and estimate how many hours you are from the closest high or low water.
- In rough terms, the tide will rise or fall its full range in six hours. A quarter of this range flows in or out in the first two hours, another quarter in the last two, with a full half rising or falling in the middle two hours, where most of the flow is concentrated.

You use this formula to calculate as follows:

Assuming an arrival time of 1600 (4pm) and a high tide at 1400 (2pm), a low tide with a height above datum of 2 feet, and a range of 12 feet, you will have had two hours of EBB (tide that is going down) at 1600. This leaves three quarters of range (9 ft.) to fall. This leaves you 9 feet, plus the height of low tide above chart datum (2 feet) plus chart soundings below chart datum (7 feet) = 18 feet, more than enough water in a calm, shallow cove. This information also helps determine the length of the anchor rode.

Now assume that you are on a 40-footer approaching the entrance to Catalina Harbor at Catalina

Figure 4-13 *Dark area of pilings indicates height of high tides.*

Island. Use the accompanying information to work out when you would need maximum scope on July 1, 1987.

One last point: remember that at low water neap tides there will be more water at low tide than at low water spring tides.

TABLE 2. — TIDAL DIFFERENCES AND OTHER CONSTANTS   171

NO.	PLACE	POSITION		DIFFERENCES				RANGES		Mean Tide Level
		Lat.	Long.	Time		Height		Mean	Diurnal	
				High water	Low water	High water	Low water			
		° ' N	° ' W	h. m.	h. m.	ft	ft	ft	ft	ft
	Santa Barbara Islands									
457	Wilson Cove, San Clemente Island........	33 00	118 33	-0 03	-0 03	*0.94	*0.94	3.6	5.2	2.7
459	Catalina Harbor, Santa Catalina Island..	33 26	118 30	+0 11	+0 17	*0.94	*0.94	3.6	5.2	2.7
461	Avalon, Santa Catalina Island...........	33 21	118 19	+0 06	+0 09	*0.96	*0.96	3.7	5.3	2.7
463	Santa Barbara Island....................	33 29	119 02	-0 02	+0 04	*0.92	*0.92	3.5	5.1	2.6
465	San Nicolas Island.....................	33 16	119 30	+0 10	+0 21	*0.88	*0.88	3.3	4.9	2.5
467	Prisoners Harbor, Santa Cruz Island.....	34 01	119 41	+0 25	+0 26	*0.90	*0.90	3.4	5.0	2.6
469	Bechers Bay, Santa Rosa Island..........	34 00	120 03	+0 37	+0 35	*0.96	*0.96	3.6	5.3	2.8
471	Cuyler Harbor, San Miguel Island........	34 03	120 21	+0 33	+0 34	*0.94	*0.94	3.5	5.2	2.7

70   LOS ANGELES (Outer Harbor), CALIFORNIA, 1987

Times and Heights of High and Low Waters

	JULY							AUGUST							SEPTEMBER					
Day	Time	Height		Day	Time	Height		Day	Time	Height		Day	Time	Height		Day	Time	Height		Day	Time	Height	
	h m	ft	m		h m	ft	m		h m	ft	m		h m	ft	m		h m	ft	m		h m	ft	m
1	0634	0.3	0.1	16	0037	4.6	1.4	1	0023	3.7	1.1	16	0353	3.1	0.9	1	1440	5.3	1.6	16	0704	3.9	1.2
W	1336	3.9	1.2	Th	0713	0.5	0.2	Sa	0626	1.6	0.5	Su	0734	2.7	0.8	Tu	2305	0.5	0.2	W	1101	3.4	1.0
	1823	2.9	0.9		1401	5.0	1.5		1326	4.8	1.5		1448	5.1	1.6						1644	4.9	1.5
	2354	4.4	1.3		2023	1.8	0.5		2027	2.0	0.6		2257	0.9	0.3								
2	0706	0.7	0.2	17	0154	3.8	1.2	2	0147	3.1	0.9	17	0623	3.3	1.0	2	0644	3.5	1.1	17	0019	0.4	0.1
Th	1415	4.1	1.2	F	0755	1.2	0.4	Su	0700	2.1	0.6	M	0900	3.1	0.9	W	0927	3.3	1.0	Th	0719	4.1	1.2
	1943	2.7	0.8		1453	5.2	1.6		1416	5.0	1.5		1602	5.2	1.6		1610	5.6	1.7		1156	3.0	0.9
					2157	1.4	0.4		2206	1.4	0.4										1740	5.2	1.6

Figure 4-14 *Lower table gives a day to day prediction of high and low tides. The upper chart indicates the time differences for nearby locations.*

Towing A Dinghy

This time you will be sailing with a dinghy towed astern. We will learn a great deal more about the dinghy in **Section 5**, but you have to secure it for towing at sea:

1. **Empty the dinghy of all gear,** including oars, PFDs, and oarlocks. Bring the outboard engine on deck and lash it in place astern.

2. **Prepare two towing lines,** leading from separate rings or securing places.

3. **Secure the dinghy alongside or at bow or stern,** close inboard, until you are clear of the slip and can tow it.

4. When in open water, **secure the tow** by bringing the dinghy astern with the two painters. Secure one to each stern cleat, giving the dinghy ample line length to be clear of stern and propeller. By distributing the load evenly, steering of the yacht remains unimpaired. Secure the dinghy BEFORE accelerating to cruising speed.

Generally speaking, charter companies send you out with a fiberglass dinghy, which is too heavy to bring on deck. Since you will almost certainly be chartering in relatively sheltered waters, you should have no problem towing, provided you give the dinghy ample tow line length to move about in a following sea.

We are now ready for our long-awaited passage. But first some quick review questions:

Figure 4-15 *A dinghy towed astern should be amply secured.*

REVIEW QUESTIONS

1. List FIVE items that should be checked before you go off on passage:

   1. _____

   2. _____

   3. _____

   4. _____

   5. _____

2. Fog forms when the dew point and air temperature coincide:

   True _____   False _____

3. Radiation fog is:

   a. Fog formed over land by cooling temperatures

   b. Fog formed over open water by cooling temperatures

   c. Fog formed over cities by smog and haze

   d. Fog formed over mountains and islands

4. You have arrived at an anchorage at 1500, with a high tide due in three hours. The water depth on the chart is 7 feet, the low tide height is 3 feet above datum, high tide height 12 feet above chart datum.

   What is the depth of water below your keel at time of arrival?
   (Your boat draws 3 1/2 feet).

5. When towing a dinghy, you use:

   a. Short tow line and one line

   b. two lines and long scope

   c. one line and long scope

   d. two lines and short scope

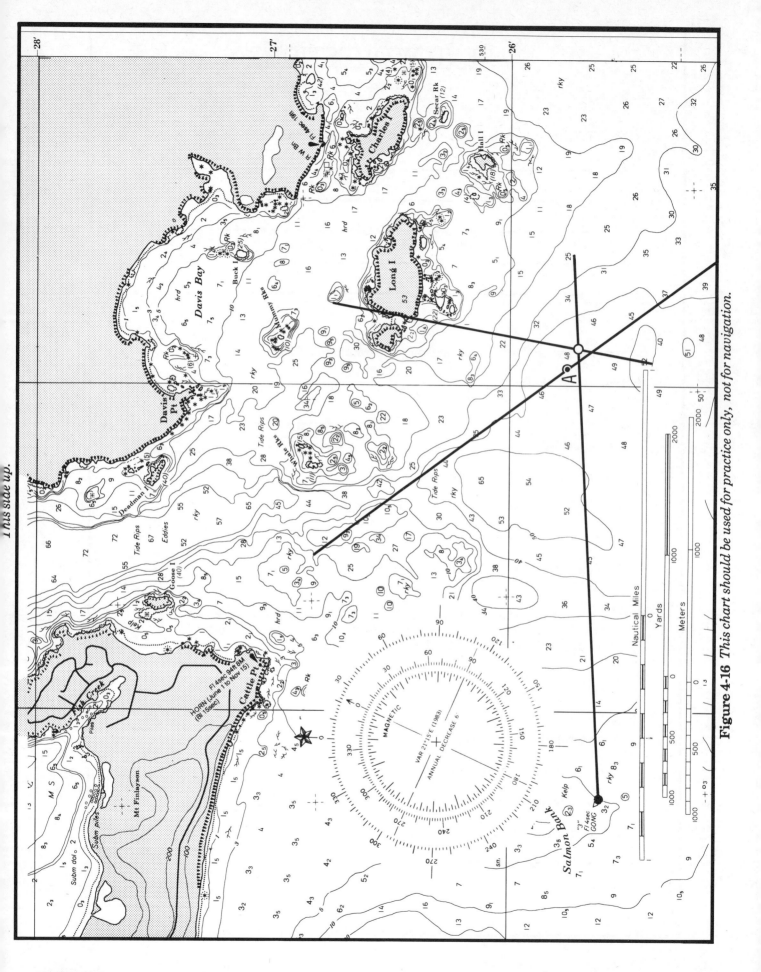

Figure 4-16 This chart should be used for practice only, not for navigation.

AFLOAT SKILLS

In this section we take an imaginary journey along the Washington coast. A special chart has been printed on the previous page. PLEASE STUDY IT CAREFULLY. Your passage will take you along the course which begins near the bottom right hand corner of the page. You have begun at a location which lies beyond the portion of the chart which is printed on the page.

For the purposes of this lesson we are making some simple assumptions. Firstly, you are operating in a location and time when tide and current have little effect on navigation. In reality, our sailing area, the entrance to San Juan Channel between San Juan and Lopez Islands, would present many navigational challenges due to tidal currents.

Secondly, you are setting out on a day with a beam wind of 12 to 15 knots. One course change is needed. You plan to sail to a sheltered cove with sandy beach, with good holding ground. However, you will need a dinghy to get ashore.

We assume you have completed your preparation and planning and are out in open water. It is time to set your course for your destination.

Setting Your Course

• The skipper checks the chart and reads off the course.
• The helmsperson brings the yacht onto said course.
• As he or she does so, the skipper takes the time and notes the reading on the knotmeter, or sets the odometer to zero.
• The skipper takes a fix, which he or she plots on the chart. This should coincide with the plotted position from where your course was laid.
• While the skipper plots the course, the crew trims sails for the correct course.

Maintaining Course

You are on your way! A wise skipper rotates helming duty regularly between crew members so that everyone has a chance to sail the boat. The skipper should check the course regularly, ensuring that the helmsperson is maintaining an accurate compass heading. Another member of the crew is delegated to keep a close lookout for other vessels, obstructions, and landmarks.

A good rule of thumb for the helm is to LOOK AROUND 360 DEGREES AT LEAST EVERY 5 MINUTES, AND UNDER THE JIB EVERY TWO OR THREE MINUTES.

Every half an hour, the skipper or navigator should read the log and plot the dead reckoning position on the chart, (see illustration labeled "A" on the chart) using this reading as the basis for doing so. The key to this exercise is computing distance, which is achieved by:

• **Reading the log,** which gives you the distance traveled as recorded by the ship's instrumentation,

• **Adding or subtracting the amount of current or tide flowing** with, or against, you (in this case assumed to be zero) to the log reading.

This computed distance, which is an estimate, is plotted along your course to give you a DEAD RECKONING POSITION (DR).

Checking this DR position is where your chosen landmarks come into play, for you can use them to check your actual speed over the water and to refine your dead reckoning. For example, after an hour's sailing, fix your position. You may find that the log says 6.5 knots, when the fix shows you have actually covered 7.0 miles over the ground. This means you are half a mile ahead of your DR. This information could be of vital importance if fog closes in suddenly. Why is the DR often inaccurate? Because very often the log, tide, current, even the compass, may be slightly inaccurate, resulting in a cumulative error for your DR.

As a rule of thumb, always know where you are to within half a mile on a charter passage. Fix your position at least every hour, and AT ONCE if visibility deteriorates and fog rolls in. This will enable you to set course for shallow water or plot a safe course if need be.

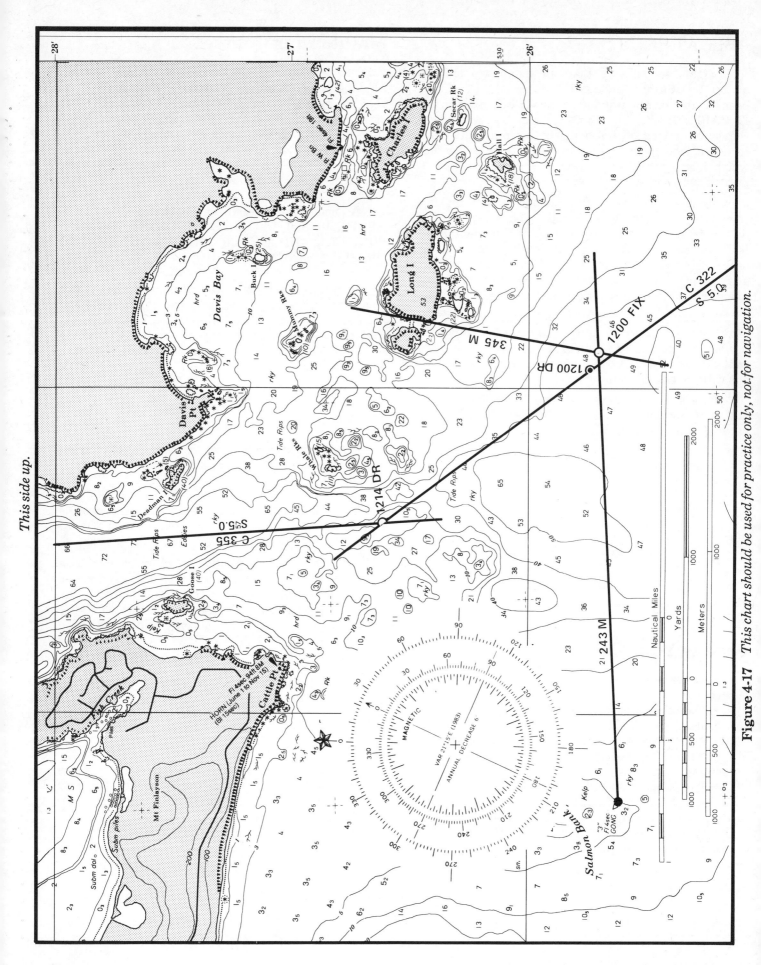

This chart should be used for practice only, not for navigation.

Figure 4-17

Turning the Corner

And so the passage proceeds smoothly with bright sunshine, a fine wind, and smooth seas; a comfortable beam reach. The coastline unfolds as you sail along. Do not be lulled into a sense of false security! Coastal pilotage requires a keen sense of direction, position, and orientation. Above all, you have to be careful to identify your landmarks precisely, for two headlands can look alike, or one could be confused for another on the basis of an imprecise description in the cruising guide.

To guard against pilotage errors, especially in tidal waters, where currents can set you off course:

• **Maintain an accurate compass course** at all times.

• **Keep your DR plot up-to-date** every 30 minutes.

By "precise landmark" we mean a lighthouse, readily identifiable structure, or a natural feature that has a specific location on a chart. For instance, a headland with no specific identifying features is probably useless for this purpose. In contrast, a buoy with a fixed position on the chart is not.

On our passage, you are now approaching the channel where you have to alter course toward your final destination.

Identifying the channel is easy enough. There is a photograph in the Coast Pilot. Furthermore, there is a small island visible between the land masses.

But are you sure that this is the right channel? With your elevation this close to sea level, land configurations often look alike. We can assume that if your DR positions have been relatively consistent with periodic fixes, you will be in the right neighborhood. Although two land masses can appear similar, they are rarely preceded by the same sequences of identifying factors. For instance, two inlets roughly 1 mile wide could exist within a few miles of one another. But on a southern approach only one would lie beyond certain radio towers, buildings, cliffs and the like. Therefore, it is important to use your chart, cruising guide and Coast Pilot to identify the stepping stones to your destination.

On our approach to Castle Point, we identified Long Island, then Mummy Rocks and Whale Rocks all to starboard. To port in the distance the Salmon Bank Light is visible. Now we check our bearing to Cattle Point as it appears on the chart. A crewman on the bow checks the actual bearing with a hand bearing compass. Our numbers match within a few degrees confirming that this is, in fact, the place we had decided to enter the channel.

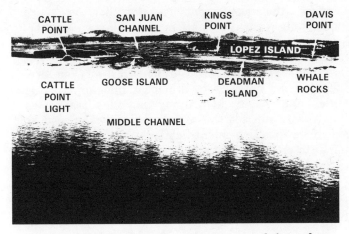

SAN JUAN AND LOPEZ ISLANDS, WASHINGTON

Figure 4-18 *This portion of a photograph from the Coast Pilot shows the channel we must enter. It may look quite a bit different than what one expects from looking only at the chart.*

Your course calls for you to alter direction from a point 3/4 of a mile offshore of Cattle Point, when the Cattle Point light bears 281 deg. magnetic.

As you approach the turning point, fix the yacht at more frequent intervals until you can work out an accurate ETA for the turning point. Using the bearing compass, check the bearing on the headland until it reads 281 deg. M. Then:

• **Alter course** to the new direction and trim sails.
• **Note the time** of course alteration and fix position of the ship to check turning point.
• **Start new DR plot** and work out ETA for destination.

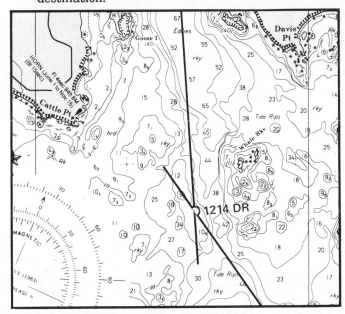

Figure 4-19 *Shows a closer view of the charted area where we must turn to enter the channel.*

Approaching the Anchorage

Now the excitement mounts, for you are approaching your destination, an unknown anchorage with unfamiliar landmarks. Your first task is to identify the anchorage from a distance. Your DR plot and fixes will tell you how far off you are. Consult your notes from the coast pilot or cruising guide, and begin identifying key landmarks as soon as you can see the coastline clearly. As soon as you have positive identifications, use these landmarks to establish the position of your vessel and the distance and course to the entrance.

If there are outlying dangers, use navigation buoys and other landmarks to skirt your way round them.

As you approach the final mile or so to the entrance and reach more sheltered water, it is time to make preparations for anchoring. IF NECESSARY, ENTER THE ANCHORAGE, STAY IN DEEP WATER AND MAKE PREPARATIONS IN SMOOTH WATER.

1. **Start engine**. Switch on depth meter.

2. **Lower sails** and secure temporarily, but leave them ready to hoist at short notice in case the engine fails. You can harbor stow them later. If you are using a hanked jib, either unhank it and stow it below, or lash the sail to the guardrail.

3. **Allocate crew to anchoring tasks**: two hands on foredeck dealing with anchor, one to relay instructions amidships, one to watch dinghy painter.

4. **Foredeck crew flake anchor chain and line on deck** and unlash anchor from bow roller ready to drop.

5. While these activities are going on, **skipper examines anchorage**. Using notes and assessment of local conditions decides where to anchor.

Figure 4-20 *When our navigation has yielded a safe entrance to the harbor of choice, a local cruising guide will provide descriptions and photographs of the anchorage area.*

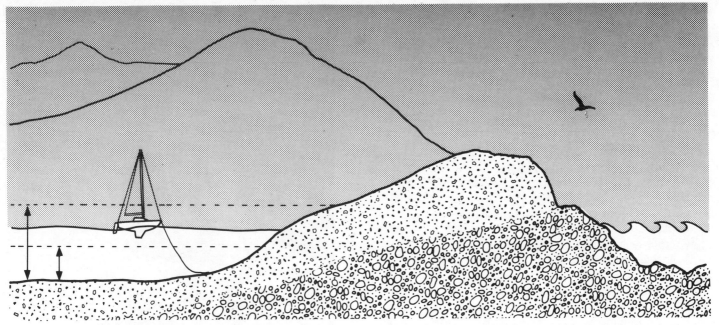

Figure 4-21 *A desirable anchorage will feature ample but not excessive depth, room to swing when the wind changes direction, shelter from wind and waves as well as good holding ground. Other attractive characteristics like available landing spots should also be taken into consideration.*

Now you enter the anchorage, taking a run through the cove at slow speed, watching both the general topography and bottom, as well as depth meter readings. Choosing where to anchor means weighing the following factors:

• **Overall shelter** provided by the anchorage, especially the land, offlying reefs, and other features both for prevailing conditions, and from other wind directions that could fill in without warning.
• **Overall shelter** provided by the anchorage from swells that are, or may, roll into the cove.
• **Depth of water** in the bay, and available swinging room.
• **Currents or tides** that might be sluicing through the anchorage.
• **Positions of other yachts** in the anchorage, if any, also of local mooring buoys.
• **Available landing spots.**
• **The holding ground** on the bottom. The best is sand and or mud; the worst rock, grass, or coral.

This list may seem confusing, but in practice, your choices will be limited and the pilot or cruising guide will give you much valuable information. In the final analysis, however, everything comes down to judgement on the spot. Pay particular attention to the principles involved; to the natural forces like wind and current acting on the yacht. If you have a thorough knowledge of these, frequent practice will soon enhance your expertise. And experience is all that separates the beginner from the expert.

You decide where to anchor, and now move out into deeper water for the final approach:

1. **Brief the crew** as to exactly how you are going to approach, and what procedure you intend to follow, including specific commands.

2. **Approach your anchoring spot head to wind,** barely moving over the ground. Warn the crew to stand by for drop anchor. Be sure to check that the bitter end of the anchor line is secured in the chain locker or on deck.

3. **Stop the bow** at the precise point where the anchor will lie. Order "Drop!"

4. **Engage reverse** as the anchor hits the bottom and rode pays out.

5. When about THREE times the depth of water of line is over the bow, **call "snub."** The foredeck hands loop the line round a bow cleat or the winch and hold tight. The boat moves astern and tensions the line, digging the anchor into the ground. When the snub is secure:

6. **Go astern slowly** and pay out more line until adequate scope is over the bow.

7. **Engage neutral and secure anchor line.** Once the vessel has settled down, take two ANCHOR BEARINGS on landmarks ashore which can be used to check your position should the wind pipe up.

8. **Stow the vessel for harbor.**

Scope

How much scope (length of anchor line) should you have over the bow? Opinions differ somewhat among experts, but here are some guidelines:

- <u>Winds below 10 knots</u>:
All chain: three times the depth of water at low tide
Chain and line: five times the same depth
- <u>Winds between 10 and 25 knots</u>:
All chain: five times the depth of water at low tide
Chain and line: seven to nine times the same depth
- <u>Winds over 25 knots</u>:
Whatever your rode, pay out everything aboard.

How do you measure the amount of rode over the bow? If you are lucky, the charter company will have marked the line every 30 to 60 feet with leather tags or fine line, using a simple code, like, say, one string indicating 30 feet, two 60 feet, and so on. If they have not, use the rode without markings first time, then make your own temporary markings with electrical tape, sufficient for you to have some idea how much is over the bow. Be sure to ask the charter company about their marking system. You might also pay the line out in distances equal to both arms extended. This length is roughly that of your height. By counting and multiplying, you can compute the length of line to go over the bow.

Figure 4-23 *Some charter yachts may use markers (shown) at designated intervals to help keep track of scope.*

Figure 4-22 *Crew at the bow secures the anchor rode to a cleat. Then, while the skipper motors in reverse, the bow crew feels the rode for dragging along the bottom.*

Laying Two Anchors

Before we stow for harbor, let us try laying two anchors, something you may have to do **when**:

• **Swinging room is restricted** by the available deep water or other yachts.
• **A strong tide flows** through a restricted anchorage, flowing from opposite directions during ebb and flood.
• You need to moor the vessel for **extra security** in very strong winds.
• **Other yachts are anchored with two anchors.**

Laying two anchors is somewhat more complicated than basic anchoring, but it gives you added security in congested anchorages and strong winds. For chartering purposes, you need to know three techniques:

- Laying anchors **bow and stern.**
- The so-called **Bahamian Moor**, where you lie to two anchors set at 180 degrees to one another, but swing on your own axis.
- Laying two **anchors at 45 deg,** to the bow.

Anchoring Fore and Aft

You anchor fore and aft in congested anchorages, or when other boats within swinging radius are anchored fore and aft. You can lay the stern anchor in two ways — either with a dinghy, or from the yacht herself.

Laying with a dinghy requires less skill on the part of the crew, and is a useful technique for beginners:

1. **Anchor the yacht with the bow anchor** in the correct position. Use the engine to keep her clear of neighboring vessels or in deep water if necessary. Lay out full scope at the bow.
2. **Bring the dinghy to the stern** and send one crew member down into her with the oars. Load the stern anchor and the length of chain that joins anchor to rode into the stern of the dinghy. Assign a crew member to pay out the remaining line from the stern of the yacht.
3. The **dinghy rows out from the stern** in the direction where the anchor is to be laid, with the skipper giving steering directions from the yacht.

Figure 4-24 *Stern crew pays out anchor rode while crew member rows anchor and chain out in the dinghy.*

4. When the correct position is reached, the anchor and chain are laid, and the crew aboard the yacht, **haul in and tension anchor line**, so that vessel is in the correct position. The correct position for a second anchor is a location with adequate depth that allows about equal scope to be laid bow and stern of the yacht. In other words, you should lay the second anchor about equidistant from the stern as the main anchor is to the bow.

You recover the anchor either by sending out the dinghy, or by paying out line from the bow until you can haul the stern anchor aboard from the yacht herself.

Figure 4-24 1/2 *An anchor windlass reduces the muscle power needed to weigh anchor*

Laying Two Anchors from the Yacht —Bow and Stern and at 45 Degrees

Laying a second anchor with the yacht herself requires good judgement and careful control of the vessel under power:

The diagrams show two ways of laying a second anchor from a vessel, over the stern or at 45 degrees from the bow.

Laying a second anchor over the stern is an alternative to using a dinghy, while you normally lay two anchors over the bow in very heavy weather, when you want to minimize the chances of dragging. You can sometimes see yachts lying to two bow anchors in very strong Bahamian northerlies of 35 knots or more. They lie in sheltered, but windswept anchorages where sand offers good holding ground.

With two anchors laid at 45 degrees to the bow, they lie comfortably, swing less, and the crew sleep well at night, knowing they will not move.

Before laying two anchors, it is essential to be prepared ahead of time. **Ready both anchors on deck**, with rodes and chains flaked on deck. **Assign crew to both anchors**. Choose your anchor spot with great care, and **make a dummy run through the anchorage** pointing out the anchor spot to the crew.

The Bahamian Moor

The Bahamian Moor is ideal for use in congested channels, where the tide reverses itself with ebb and flow, or whenever you want to swing within your own length. The name probably originated in the Bahamas, where this technique is much used.

This time you lay two anchors at 180 degrees to one another, but bring the rodes to the bow, so that the yacht swings in her own length. The diagram shows you the basic procedure. Again, make sure that you prepare both anchors and assign crew members to their tasks ahead of time.

Armed with these basic anchoring techniques, you can cope with all anchoring situations you are likely to encounter when bareboating.

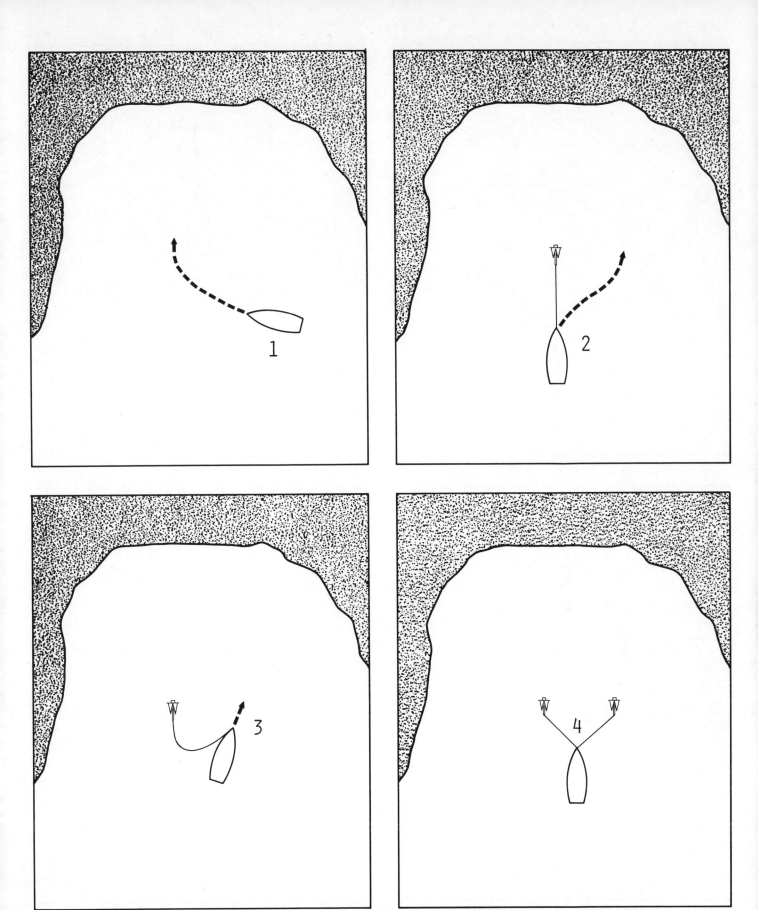

Figure 4-25 *(1). The Boat approaches a designated sight to drop the first anchor. (2).With the first anchor set, a position for the second anchor is determined. (3).The boat moves ahead to the drop sight for the second anchor taking care not to foul the first anchor's rode. (4). Finally the boat sets and adjusts the scope of the second anchor just as it did for the first anchor.*

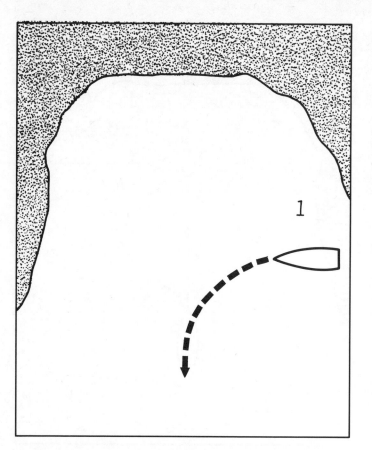

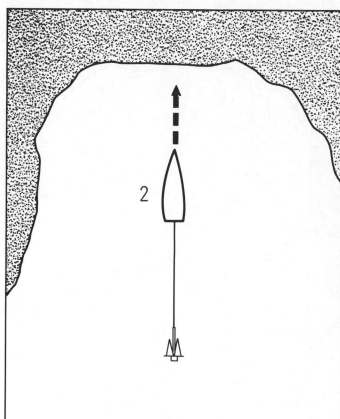

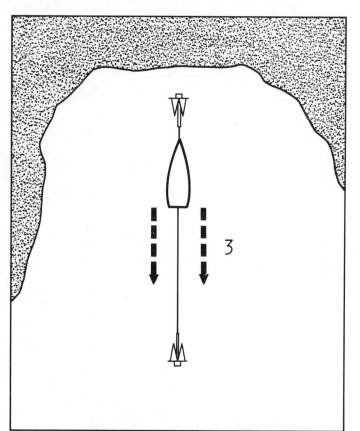

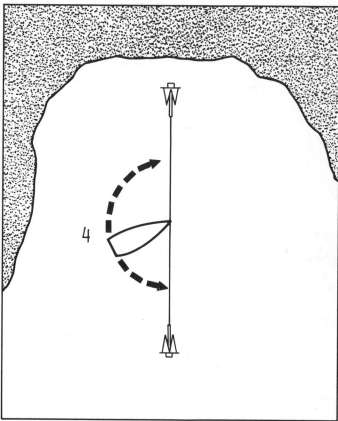

Figure 4-26 *(1). The boat approaches a designated spot to drop the first anchor. (2). A crew member walks the anchor rode to the stern and pays out rode as the boat moves forward, setting the anchor in the process. (3). The second anchor is dropped and set off the bow. The helmsman backs away from the second anchor while crew members pull in on the first anchor's rode. (4). When both anchors are set, the boat will remain virtually stationary in any wind direction.*

Harbor Stow

Now that we have finally anchored safely, it is time to stow the boat for port. Here, as with everything else in cruising, opinions differ as to how thoroughly you should stow at anchor. Here is a check list for even the most thorough skipper:

• **Check cleating and leads of anchor lines.** Install padding at fairleads to guard against chafe if necessary. Coil surplus line on deck, or in the anchor locker.
• **Stow mainsail on boom,** secure with ties, and cover. (Some skippers, including the author, prefer to keep the cover off in case you need the sail in a hurry). Coil mainsheet.
• **Unhank jib and stow in bag,** if roller furler not fitted. Coil sheets and stow away, or tension and coil at rail if roller-furler installed. Having the jib lying on deck makes anchoring difficult.
• **Coil all loose lines** and stow away. Rig awning or Bimini cover if necessary.
• **Rig swimming ladder.**
• **Lower outboard** and gear into dinghy and secure astern.
• **Turn off electronics, check Battery Switch to "1" or "2".**
• **Stow away navigation gear and complete log entry** (if appropriate).

In **Section 5,** we discuss living aboard, and life at anchor. So we now skip the hours at anchor, and deal briefly with the return passage after your night afloat.

Figure 4-27 *Bow rollers and fairleads help prevent chafing of anchor rode.*

Raising Anchor

Preparations for the return passage are identical to those discussed earlier. When everything is ready, it is time to practice raising anchor. Here is a common procedure for doing so:

1. **Skipper starts engine, assigns crew** members to specific tasks. Two hands are on the foredeck, one relays signals from bow to stern, a third guards dinghy painter. The crew remove mainsail cover and attach the main halyard if necessary.

Figure 4-28 *Use arm and leg muscles when raising anchor.*

2. **Slow ahead,** foredeck hands haul in scope on anchor line and stow same in chain locker. The skipper varies engine revolutions to allow for gusts. One bow hand signals left, right, and straight on so skipper can adjust the ship's heading.
   In strong gusts, the anchor hands take a turn with the line round the bow cleat and hold on until the tension slackens.
3. When the vessel is directly above the anchor, foredeck crew advise skipper. He or she takes a last look round, then orders them to **haul away.**
4. **Anchor is jerked** out of the ground and hauled to stemhead.
5. As soon as the anchor is off the ground, the **skipper steers the yacht** to port or starboard, whichever way gives a clear course. If necessary, the yacht is kept stationary until the anchor is secured.
6. Foredeck crew **stow line and lash down anchor in bow roller.** Alternatively, stow it in the anchor locker.

The Return Passage

The return passage is the reverse of the earlier one, except that the instructor will tell you to sail a different course, perhaps with two or three course changes on the return leg.

At least one of these new courses should be a windward one, so you can practice passage-making to windward, where you have to judge the effect of each tack. Almost certainly, the wind direction will favor one tack over the other, perhaps the inshore tack, perhaps the other. How will this affect your navigational strategy? Will you be able to clear obstructions off a headland or those outlying rocks? You will learn how important an accurate DR plot can be.

Lee-Bowing

There is one important trick you should learn, just in case you ever have to beat to windward in tidal waters. This is a situation where the tide is flowing in such a way that you are tacking to windward with the tide flowing against your lee bow. THIS MEANS THAT IT PUSHES YOU BODILY TO WINDWARD. This can make an important difference in narrow channels or on long tacks offshore in tidal waters. Do everything you can to bring the tide on your lee bow. It can pay handsome dividends.

Figure 4-29 *Current on the lee bow while beating can help push your yacht in the direction of its destination.*

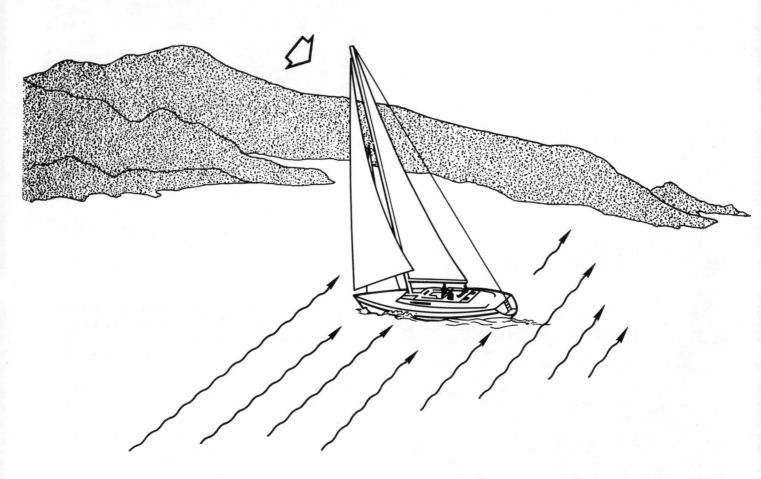

Current Insets

We stress that it is vital you keep an accurate DR plot when passage making. Sometimes, unexpected local currents can carry you inshore without warning, especially into bays or onto sub-surface reefs. Such insets are difficult to predict, making an accurate DR plot essential in any waters where you suspect such phenomena.

Temporary Anchorages

On the return passage, think about temporary anchorages, too. There may be occasions where you want to stop for lunch, for some snorkeling, or for sleep. Perhaps there is an adverse tide against you for three hours, or you are waiting for the wind to drop. Under these circumstances, it is sometimes possible to find temporary anchorage in a place that would be unacceptable for a longer stay. Try and venture into such an anchorage for a moment, so you can see what we mean. Here are some criteria for choosing temporary anchorages:

- **Adequate temporary shelter** from the prevailing wind and swell. This should be sufficient for safety and greater comfort than you would experience by heaving-to at sea.
- **Good holding ground**. sufficient depth, and adequate space to swing.
- **Ample space to clear out** in a hurry if necessary.

You will find that you will use many temporary anchorages over the years, to have lunch, to swim, or just to relax. It is advisable to learn how to choose them at an early stage, so that you never lose the

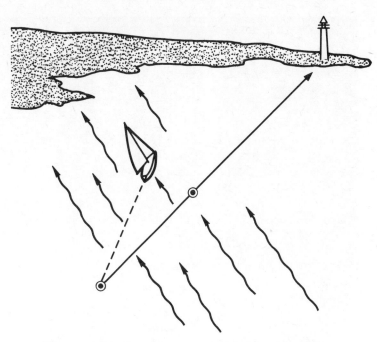

Figure 4-30 *Current can seriously interfere with progress to your destination. While steering for the lighthouse the yacht above ends up quite a distance inshore due to current.*

chance to enjoy unique, unusual places, and so add to the enjoyment of your charter.

As you come into port at the end of your passage, you will feel a great sense of satisfaction and accomplishment. This is what makes chartering such a wonderful way of life.

In **Section 5**, we will round off the course with a lesson on living aboard and some of the systems that make you comfortable.

Figure 4-31 *Temporary anchorages usually share some of the desirable characteristics of a good overnight anchorage, but remaining all night could prove uncomfortable or dangerous.*

Figure 5-1

SECTION 5

LIVING ABOARD
AND LIFE AT ANCHOR

ASHORE KNOWLEDGE

Section 5 should be taken in close conjunction with **Section 4**, where you make a 48-hour passage. During your period at anchor, you will exercise many of the skills described in this final section of the charter course. In **Section 5** you learn about water supplies and provisioning, about heads and stoves, about precautions and crew safety at anchor, and about that most essential of all equipment - the dinghy. We end with some common emergencies that can arise during a charter - going aground, springing a leak, and ropes fouling your propeller.

When you have completed **Section 5**, you will be ready for your ASA certification examination, the test of skills you have learned in this course.

LIVING ABOARD

Water Supplies

Several times in earlier sections we have referred to filling water tanks, but we have never discussed water supplies aboard. We have reserved this discussion until now because water forms an integral part of provisioning a vessel for a charter.

Your charter yacht will have large water tanks, often larger than is normal for a vessel of this size. Charter companies have found from experience that such tankage is needed to allow not only for normal domestic requirements, but for frequent fresh water showers as well; welcome refreshers after a snorkeling or swimming session.

Typical charter yacht water tanks carry between 120 and 200 gallons. You leave base with full tanks and can return to have them filled as often as you like. But why go to the trouble when you can avoid such effort by conserving water on a day-by-day

basis? The first and most golden rule of living aboard is:

FRESH WATER IS LIKE GOLD; TREAT IT AS SUCH!

If you are concerned about the purity of drinking water aboard, you might want to buy some bottled water from the supermarket for drinking purposes.

Figure 5-2 *Water tank fillers are usually on deck and clearly labeled.*

Fresh Water Systems

Your vessel has a complex fresh water system that divides into two components:

- Galley water supply
- Shower and wash basin supply

Every modern charter yacht has a pressure water system that is driven by an electrical pump fueled by the ship's batteries. This system is turned on and off by a master switch on the main electrical panel. Turn this switch on to activate the entire system.

A pressure water system means that the system pumps water when you turn on the faucets, and will keep running until you turn it off, just like ashore. This is an immediate invitation to waste water. So, as soon as you step aboard, teach your crew the following conservation measures.

- **Turn off the master switch** on the main panel unless the system is in use.
- **Last person to use the system turns off the master switch at night.**
- When washing hands, **fill basin; do not just run faucet**. Also, when washing teeth, fill a mug with water for rinsing.
- Take short showers, **turning off shower head as you soap** your wet body.
- Where possible, **use salt water for basic cleaning and cooking.**

Some of your crew may complain that domestic soap does not lather in salt water. The answer is liquid detergent, which does. Invest in a plastic bottle that is kept in the galley for both dishes and people.

Most charter yachts are fitted with hot water systems, also activated by the pressure water pump. The water is heated either by the shore power, if such a feature is fitted, or by the heat exchanger on the engine. The hot water heater itself is normally located in a cockpit locker or the engine room. If this malfunctions, you will have to contact the charter company, as this is a sealed unit.

Unless you spend your charter tied up to slips, you will need to run the engine regularly to maintain a hot water supply. Since the charter company will recommend that you do this to charge batteries and the refrigerator every day, you should have regular hot water.

Figure 5-3 *Hot water can usually be heated by the engine or with shore power.*

Most pressure water systems are relatively trouble free, but you can experience three potential problems:

- **Persistent blipping** of the pump to maintain pressure while the system is switched on but not actually being run. This hints at a leak in the plumbing. Check pipe joints throughout and repair if necessary.
- **Dribbling flow from a specific faucet**. This may be due to blockage in the filter at the faucet itself. Remove filter from orifice and clean.
- **System fails to pump** when main switch is activated. This signals either a blown fuse, a defective pump, or, if the pump runs but nothing happens, a punctured water pump diaphragm. The company may provide you with spares, in which case the replacement of the offending part is an easy matter. Be sure, however, to ask the charter co. about this before you leave.
- **One tank may be empty.** Check water levels in your tanks, then use the gate valves in the bilge to switch to a full tank. The charter company will show you where these are located.

Most pressure systems have manual backup pumps, at least in the galley. These may be of the hand operated type, or a foot pump, with the pedals by the cabin sole. These bring water to the sink through **a special faucet.**

Most systems drain sinks by gravity through special sea cocks. Be patient, for drainage may be slower than at home. The water has a shorter distance to gain momentum and a smaller diameter pipe to run through than in your kitchen. A few yachts have special electrical pumps for the purpose, which are self explanatory.

Showers

Every yacht of any size has a shower these days. Many charter yachts have special fiberglass lined shower compartments, on the argument that such space is easier to keep clean, with the resultant spray separated from the rest of the head. In most instances, however, the shower is an integral part of the head compartment, with the shower head on a flexible hose mounted on a bulkhead. You can remove this to shower yourself, adjusting the water temperature with the sink controls. Here is the usual procedure for the controls:

1. **Turn on sink faucets** and adjust temperature to desired level.
2. **Remove shower head** from mounting and point into sink.
3. **Turn on shower valve.** This is either a small lever by the faucets, or, more often, a push-pull fitting on the head itself.
4. **Run water through hose** until hot water reaches your hand. Use shower, controlling water flow with valve until you have finished.
5. **Turn off shower valve** and faucets.

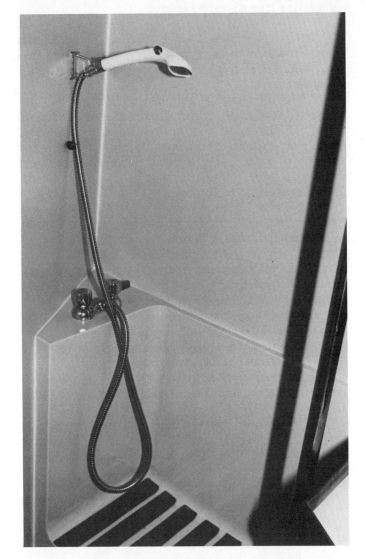

Figure 5-5 *Some kind of shower is usually found in the head compartments.*

The water drains into the base of the shower compartment and into a special basin in the bilge. Having had a shower, it is important to drain the dirty water. Most yachts have a special shower drain switch, which is activated by a waterproof switch close to the sink, often labeled "sump." When all the water has drained into the basin, activate this switch and run it until it sucks dry. A few yachts run shower water into the bilge, so you will have to run the main bilge pump.

Needless to say, the responsible crew member wipes down the shower after use, including toilet, sink, walls, so that the next person using the compartment does not get a shower, too.

Most head compartments are well ventilated. However, it is advisable to open the window port to let steam out, if possible.

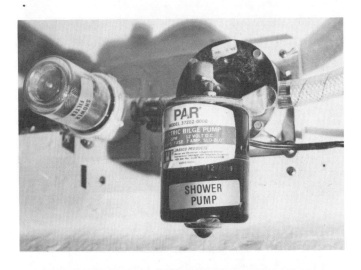

Figure 5-4 *A typical electric water pressure pump.*

Water Consumption

On longer charters it is best to calculate the water consumption per day per crew member, so that you will have some idea how long your water supplies will last.

When figuring water consumption, you are concerned not with washing, except for teeth and faces, for the crew can always take a salt water shower on a short-term basis. What matters is the amount of water people need to survive, cooking, drinking, and fulfilling basic hygiene needs. Many centuries of experience has shown that a figure between 2 quarts and 2 gallons a day is a realistic range, with the high consumption coming in tropical latitudes, where body water loss is higher. To calculate your water capacity, calculate:

Water tank capacity divided by number of crew, divided in turn by 2 gallons a day = number of days' water supply available for entire crew.

For instance: 200 gallons of water divided by a crew of four = 50 gallons per person.

50 gallons divided by 2 gallons/day = 25 days.

You can make a passage of 25 days.

Since your charter will rarely, if ever, exceed 14 days, you have plenty of reserve for showers in this case.

Many charter yachts have a salt water pump in the galley, which is useful for washing dishes and other tasks. Be careful, however, not to use this when you are in a dirty harbor or anchorage.

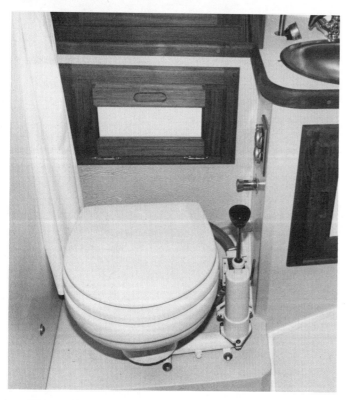

Figure 5-6 *Many heads use a hand operated pump and intake valve.*

The Head

Beyond emergency gear, there is only one other piece of ship's equipment that everyone must know how to operate. This is the ship's head. Living as you are in close quarters, it is essential that everyone use the toilets correctly, to minimize not only offending others, but malfunctions of the most unpleasant piece of equipment to repair on board.

In some cruising areas like the Great Lakes, through-hull discharges are prohibited, and your head will discharge into a special holding tank filled with chemicals that treat the waste. You then pump this out regularly at designated pumping stations, normally at gas docks. In sea-going charter areas, through-hull discharges are normal. Discharge of waste is only permitted more than three miles from coastal areas.

Whichever system you have, the head itself normally operates in the same way. Although each design varies slightly, most have two controls at the side of the seat:

- **A pumping lever** disposing of waste.
- **A smaller lever or valve** that controls the water intake to the basin.

A few types have the two controls combined in one, but for training purposes, we will assume two controls:

1. Before use, **check sea cocks are open**. There are two - one for water intake, the other the outlet, a larger diameter pipe. (If using a holding tank installation, check exit valve is open).
2. **Turn on water** intake valve at head. This device may be a switch or valve labeled "Dry" or "Flush". Pump a few times to prime the water intake.
3. After use, pump waste through the pipe with pumping lever, using steady, firm pumps.
4. After about a dozen strokes, **turn off water intake** valve. Continue pumping to clean and further flush bowl. Be sure to pump enough to expel all waste from the outlet pipe.
5. **Clean bowl** with brush or toilet paper, using water pumped into bowl.
6. **Turn off water control valve and pump dry.**
7. **Turn off sea cocks** if necessary (normally only at sea) to avoid flooding.

DO NOT PUT ANYTHING DOWN THE HEAD EXCEPT TOILET PAPER.

Paper towels, hair pins, sanitary napkins, and any other form of foreign object are anathema to marine heads, and will soon block it. Many charter companies will make you disassemble it or charge you if foreign objects are found in the mechanism. If you obey this simple rule, you should have no trouble with the head.

Malfunctions of the head can be due to:

• **Blockage of outlet pipe.** Check sea cock is open, then use a plunger to suction out blockage (most yachts provide one). In extreme circumstances, send a swimmer over the side with a wire clothes hanger to work on the seacock from outside. If these measures fail, you will have to dismantle the pipe (ugh!).

• **Pump fails to operate.** The pump gasket is probably worn out. This simply requires fitting a replacement part, if such is carried. However, this defect is rare, since most companies check this regularly.

• Water fails to flow into basin. Check sea cock, then function of the intake valve. This may just need lubricating.

If everyone uses the head properly, you are unlikely to have trouble during your charter.

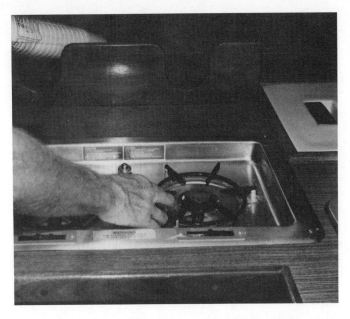

Figure 5-7 *Priming an alcohol stove burner.*

Stove and Galley

The stove is the most important piece of equipment in the galley — and the one that offers the greatest potential for fire and other accidents. Again, it behooves the prudent skipper to ensure that every crew member knows how to operate it and how to deal with sudden emergencies.

Charter yachts rely on two principal fuel supplies for their stoves: alcohol and bottled gas (LPG or propane).

Alcohol is far less common now than in years gone by. Here are a few points of interest.

1. First locate the storage tank and make sure that it contains fuel, has been pressurized and has its valve opened. DO NOT OPEN TANK WHEN IT HAS BEEN PRESSURIZED. Operating instructions or charter company personnel will explain pressurizing procedure.

2. Then we must **prime the burner.** Identify a knob, its corresponding burner and the drip cup under the burner.

3. **Turn the knob counter clockwise** until a small amount of fuel escapes into the cup.

4. Then **turn the knob clockwise** until dripping stops.

5. **Light the fuel in the cup** and allow it to burn for at least five to ten minutes. The resulting lazy flames heat the burner allowing it to operate properly. Many alcohol fires are caused by a flare up from an inadequately warmed-up burner that shoots liquid fuel into the air. Be sure to heat the burner adequately before turning on control again.

6. **Turn the knob counter clockwise again.** The resulting flames should more resemble those of a gas stove at home than the flames we saw while preheating. Alcohol flames are often practically invisible, especially in bright light. Be careful not to let lighted fuel spatter. It could land on your hand or face without your being aware of it.

7. **Turn off burner by turning knob clockwise.** Avoid leaving pressure in the tank for extended periods of time.

Alcohol fires can be dowsed with water, so keep a pan of it handy whenever lighting the stove.

Figure 5-8 *Keeping a saucepan of water over a burner as you light it helps prevent flare-ups.*

To minimize the risk of alcohol fires:
- **Never overfill the burner cup when priming.**
- **Never reprime a hot burner.** Allow it to cool first.
- **Always keep a pan full of water over a burner** as you light it. This will reduce the impact of a flare-up if one occurs.

All bottled gasses are highly flammable, but propane is especially hazardous, since it is heavier than air. This means that a propane leak will discharge gas into the bottom of your bilge, with grave risk of an explosion if someone lights a match anywhere aboard. This is why propane stoves are so carefully installed and their bottles vented overboard from the cockpit. This is also why propane gas has an unpleasant odor — so you know you have a leak at once.

Every propane stove has a set of switches that guard against leaks when not in use. Here is the typical starting procedure:

1. **Turn on gas supply** at the bottle. This is a turn-valve by the pressure gauge on top of the cylinder in the special gas locker in the cockpit. As you turn it on, check for a gas odor. There should be none.
2. If necessary, **turn on "stove" switch** on main electrical panel. This is unnecessary on most yachts.
3. **Turn on Gas Solenoid Switch** by main electrical panel. This is a special switch that controls the flow of gas to the stove, and typically has a red light that glows when the system is on. If this fails to come on, first check the fuse, if one is installed. If this is operating correctly, the solenoid is probably faulty (a new unit will be required). Call the charter company.
4. Operate stove like a gas stove at home.

Always keep a crew member stationed in the galley when stove or oven is operating. Turn burners off immediately if flame goes out accidentally.

The oven controls on a yacht stove are usually somewhat different. Proceed as follows:

1. **Activate stove system** as above.
2. **Open oven door** and locate pilot light outlet by gas burner. This is probably under a small hatch in the oven floor.
3. **Turn oven control knob** to "pilot" and hold lighted match to pilot light outlet. Pilot flame will ignite. Home models require that the knob be depressed while pilot is lit.
4. **Allow pilot light to burn** for at least 30 seconds.
5. **Close oven door** and set required baking temperature. Oven burner will ignite after a short interval.

To turn off the stove, reverse the procedure. BE SURE TO TURN OFF THE GAS SUPPLY AT THE CYLINDER AFTER USE.

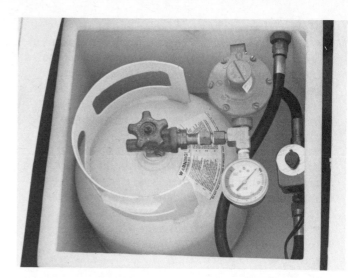

Figure 5-9 *Propane tanks are usually stored in a locker on deck.*

Figure 5-10 *Propane tank valves should be kept closed unless tanks are in use.*

Figure 5-11 *Oven pilot setting.*

Galley Emergencies

Galley emergencies can be especially hazardous because they happen so suddenly. Here are simple procedures for dealing with some common problems:

Gas leaks usually betray themselves with a strong smell of propane. If your yacht is fitted with an electrical bilge sniffer, it sounds an alarm if gas permeates the boat.

1. **Extinguish all cigarettes or other bare flames** at once, also **turn off gas supply**.
2. **Send everyone on deck** and forward, if possible into the dinghy or ashore.
3. **Turn off the electrical system** and engine if running.
4. **Open all hatches** and ventilate boat until gas is dispersed.
5. **Locate source of leak** and correct problem. At this point, disconnect cylinders from supply.

Gas leaks can be located by putting soapy water on all connections. If the mixture bubbles, you have a leak. Most such faults are due to faulty packing of pipe joints. Call the charter company, or repack the joint with plumber's tape or pipe dope, if aboard.

Galley fires pose two immediate problems - the fire itself and the burns resulting from same.

Fires usually stem from fuel igniting and burners flaring up, a common problem with alcohol stoves (dealt with above), or from grease igniting in a pan.

Small grease fires are best put out by smothering them with a suitable cloth, thereby starving them of oxygen. If there is the slightest danger of flames spattering, use the galley fire extinguisher, which is rated for both paper and fat fires.

Every crew member should know where the fire extinguishers aboard are located and how they are operated. However, if there is time, quickly consider alternatives to using fire extinguishers to dowse the flames. The mess is horrendous to clean up afterwards.

Sometimes a careless smoker or an ignited match thrown into the garbage will start a fast flaring fire. Such fires can quickly be extinguished by throwing the container overboard - but you have to be quick. Otherwise use water or the fire extinguisher.

To minimize the risk of galley fires:
• **Always extinguish matches** by dipping them in water before putting them in the garbage.
• **Cover frying pans**, especially when cooking at sea.
• **Check carefully and regularly for gas leaks.**
• **Always turn off stove fuel supply** and solenoid switches after use.
• **Restrict smoking** in the galley.

Figure 5-12 *Soapy water being applied to gas tubing joint.*

Figure 5-13 *Dip matches in water before tossing them into the trash.*

Preventing Scalding and Burns

The danger of scalds and burns is never totally absent when cooking, even ashore. The risks are increased one hundredfold on a charter, especially if you are cooking under way. Most commonly, burns occur when a sudden lurch sends a frying pan sliding and fat spattering onto someone's hands. In the tropics, a cook in shorts and nothing else stands severe risk of catastrophic scalding on the chest. Once again, you can minimize the risk by taking some elementary precautions:

- **Never, even in the hottest weather, cook without a shirt.**
- **Wear an apron** or protective clothing that covers as much of your upper body as possible.
- **Use oven gloves** when handling hot pans. Many scalds and burns result from unthinking handling of hot handles.
- **Cover frying pans** at all times, also pots full of boiling water.
- In a seaway, **wear foul weather gear** to protect you against hot spillage.
- When making long passages, **precook as many dishes as possible**, to minimize cooking times and elaborate food preparation.

Figure 5-14 *Always wear protective clothing while cooking afloat.*

Refrigerator

A refrigerator makes all the difference between comfort and discomfort aboard a charter yacht, especially in the tropics. Try to charter a boat that has a large fridge. It will enable you to carry many more fresh provisions, enough for two weeks or more. Besides, doesn't everyone like their drinks cold!

Most fridges have cold plates that freeze food placed next to them solid, leaving you space to put vegetables, beer, and other necessities elsewhere in the cold compartment. A few large yachts also have separate freezer compartments.

The controls for yacht fridges are simplicity itself, and need no special instructions. What is important, however, is that you remember that the fridge is run off the ship's batteries. As such, it can drain them rapidly if you run the fridge without using the engine at the same time. This is why charter companies recommend you run the engine for at least two hours a day. Be sure to check this with your charter co. before you start off.

When packing a yacht refrigerator, be sure to put foods that should be kept frozen in the coldest parts of the box, preferably in the order in which you might need them. The most frequently used foods and drinks should be stored in the most accessible part of the box.

Provisioning Ship

A charter vacation is a magic time when you forget the tyrannies of shoreside diets and austere living. Eat well, and enjoy good living as you break loose from the real world!

Some people go all out and ship out with gourmet foods, like Chicken Kiev or Steak Tartare. Others prefer simpler diets. Provisioning is such a matter of personal preference that one can only make some general recommendations here.

In many charter areas, especially in the Caribbean, charter companies offer special provisioning packages at a fixed rate per day. These include the ingredients for breakfast and lunch, as well as snacks. "Full provisioning" provides all dinners as well, "partial provisions" includes only a few, or none at all, on the assumption that you will eat ashore sometimes. Since you probably will, and the package contains too much food anyhow, always go for the partial package.

If you charter in an area where provisioning packages are available, purchase them. You will pay a flat rate per person, per day. This will save time and perhaps money. After all, you are not going on vacation to go grocery shopping!

If you have to do your own provisioning, follow whatever meal plan your crew prefers, and make up menus on the basis of discussions with them.

Some general guidelines:

• Remember **people eat more on the water** and tend to snack more frequently. Plenty of nourishing snacks and candy bars are a good idea.

• **Plan on a relatively leisurely and hearty breakfast**, invariably a picnic lunch, perhaps one where people make their own sandwiches, and a more elaborate dinner.

• Check to see if the yacht provides an **over-the-stern barbeque**. Plan on using it as much as possible, to keep the cabin cool.

Figure 5-15

• If you plan much passage-making, **shop for dishes that can be cooked in advance** and then be quickly heated under way. In planning your menus, stock up on fresh fruit and vegetables, low-fat foods and fiber. Avoid greasy foods as much as possible: they are disastrous for sea-sick-prone crew members.

• Carry canned staples, and try and buy fresh food every few days if this is feasible.

Drinking preferences vary widely from crew to crew. The following are excellent for passage-making:
- plain bottled water,
- orange and other still fruit juices,
- hot tea and coffee, caffeinated or decaffeinated,
- hot chocolate or hot cocoa,

Many skippers outlaw liquor while under passage and discourage carbonated drinks at sea on the grounds that they can agitate peoples' stomachs. Remember that every state has laws relating to drinking and the operating of boats that can be as stringent as those relating to automobiles.

One last point about provisioning: if your yacht has no refrigerator, plan to buy only small quantities of perishable foods like fresh meat, milk, and vegetables. You should aim to replenish supplies at each port, when you also stock up on ice. Be sure to select impact-resistant packaging. Glass bottles should be avoided if possible.

Activities at Anchor

EVEN AT ANCHOR, THE SKIPPER ASSUMES RESPONSIBILITY FOR THE CREW'S SAFETY. This responsibility need not be onerous, if everyone uses their common sense. Here are some points to look out for:

• **Children and non-swimmers should wear PFDs** at all times when on deck or in the dinghy.

• **No one under the influence of alcohol should operate the dinghy.**

• **No one should swim without someone on deck watching.**

• When crew members go ashore, **the skipper should know where they are going**, and roughly how long they will be away.

• **Everyone should know how to operate the dinghy**, and how to secure it properly ashore.

• **Any crew member left aboard alone should know how to operate the engine** and what to do if the anchor drags in an emergency.

• **Work out a recall system** using the fog horn. For instance, one blast could mean "return on board in ten minutes," repeated blasts an emergency recall of all hands. Be sure your system cannot become confused with internationally recognized distress and fog signals.

Figure 5-16

Swimming and Swimming Precautions

Swimming and snorkeling are two of the great pleasures of a charter cruise, and some elementary precautions can add immeasurably to both safety and enjoyment. **Some swimming precautions:**

• **Determine whether it is safe to swim** in the anchorage. Some potential hazards: cold water temperatures that could induce hypothermia, sharks, underwater obstructions, and fast-running tides or currents. The sailing directions may give you guidance, or local people or neighboring yachts. Currents can be determined by observation. If people swim in fast running water, trail a line with a life ring astern of the yacht, so a swimmer can grab it. Have the dinghy ready to use at short notice under such conditions.

• **Rig a boarding ladder** or secure line for safe reboarding, especially for children.

• **Check peoples' swimming ability** carefully.

• **Have someone on deck** whenever people are swimming, just in case.

• **Cover all open wounds** with Band Aids. Blood attracts fish.

Snorkeling can be carried out from the yacht, or more likely from the dinghy. In both instances, the precautions are much the same:

• People should **always snorkel in pairs**, even if one remains in the dinghy.

• **Take body covering** and suntan lotion in the dinghy.

• **Bring life jackets for each person** aboard.

• **Anchor the dinghy securely**, and snorkel in her immediate vicinity.

• **Do not stay in the water too long**, for creeping cold will weaken your swimming ability.

• **Always know where the other snorkler is.**

Figure 5-17

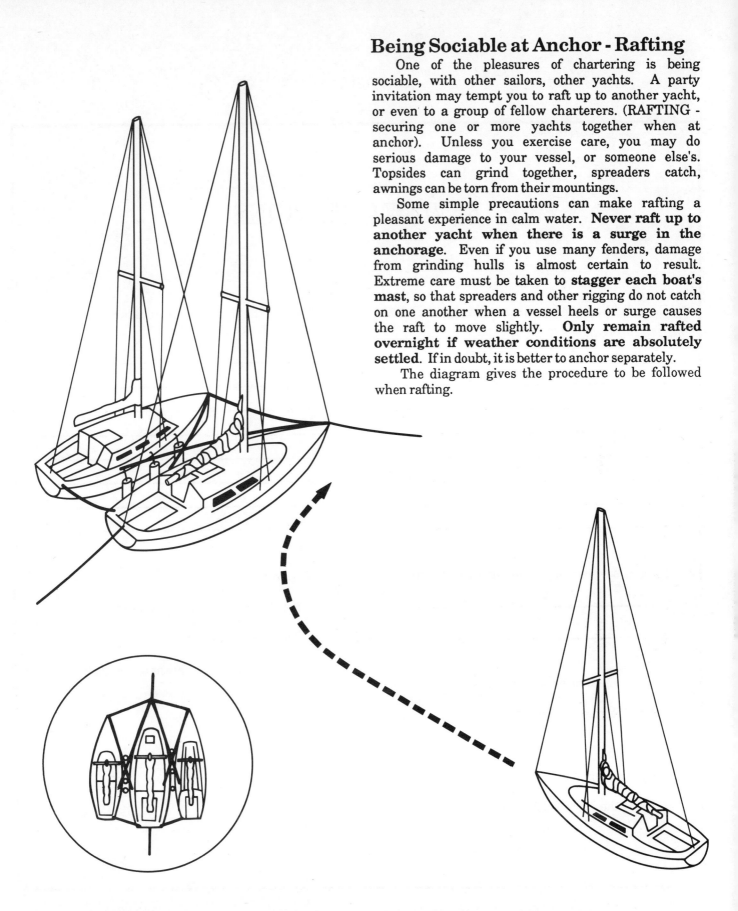

Being Sociable at Anchor - Rafting

One of the pleasures of chartering is being sociable, with other sailors, other yachts. A party invitation may tempt you to raft up to another yacht, or even to a group of fellow charterers. (RAFTING - securing one or more yachts together when at anchor). Unless you exercise care, you may do serious damage to your vessel, or someone else's. Topsides can grind together, spreaders catch, awnings can be torn from their mountings.

Some simple precautions can make rafting a pleasant experience in calm water. **Never raft up to another yacht when there is a surge in the anchorage**. Even if you use many fenders, damage from grinding hulls is almost certain to result. Extreme care must be taken to **stagger each boat's mast**, so that spreaders and other rigging do not catch on one another when a vessel heels or surge causes the raft to move slightly. **Only remain rafted overnight if weather conditions are absolutely settled**. If in doubt, it is better to anchor separately.

The diagram gives the procedure to be followed when rafting.

Figure 5-18 *The largest yacht anchors and acts as the center of the raft. Other yachts secure alongside making sure their spreaders are staggered and plenty of fenders and spring lines are used. Inset shows the completed raft.*

REVIEW QUESTIONS

1. Describe the procedure for pumping out the head.

   _____
   _____
   _____
   _____
   _____
   _____
   _____
   _____

2. Name TWO ways of putting out an alcohol fire:

   1. _____

   2. _____

3. Before swimming at anchor you should:

   a. Drink a glass of cold water

   b. Put on sun tan lotion

   c. Rig a boarding ladder

   d. Bring the dinghy alongside

4. Describe the step-by-step procedure for lighting a propane stove.

   _____
   _____
   _____
   _____
   _____
   _____
   _____

5. When rafting, you:

   a. Put the smallest yachts in the middle

   b. Put all masts in line

   c. Rig spring lines to prevent fore and aft movement

AFLOAT SKILLS

This part of Section 5 covers the dinghy, then deals with some common emergency situations that you might encounter on charter.

Dinghies

Every charter yacht is provided with a dinghy, normally between 9 and 12 feet long, depending on the size of the vessel. Most are fiberglass designs, capable not only of being rowed, but of carrying a fairly powerful outboard as well. For the purposes of this lesson, we assume you are using a fiberglass dinghy.

Figure 5-19 *The dinghy's gear should be checked just as carefully as the yacht's.*

Dinghy Gear

When using the dinghy, you should have the following equipment aboard:
- **Oars and oarlocks**. Never leave the ship without these, in case the outboard goes wrong.
- **Bailer** attached to the dinghy with a length of line.
- **Life vests** for everyone aboard.
- **Outboard motor and fuel**, usually in a separate tank.
- **Sheer pin for outboard**. This should be taped to the handle.

Outboard motor

Outboards thrive on hard work and will absorb a great deal of punishment provided you treat them right. This means taking the correct safety precautions to ensure the engine is never dunked. If the engine is of the two stroke variety, be sure to use a proper mix of oil and gas. A four stroke needs only gas in the tank. Oil is added to the crankcase.

As we have already described, the outboard should be kept on its stern pulpit bracket when you are on passage. When lowering or hoisting it to or from the dinghy, always have a crew member on deck with a safety line on the engine and someone in the dink to collect it or pass it up. The engine should not only be clamped on the dinghy stern, it must be secured to the loop in the transom with the safety line provided. This prevents it from jumping over the side if the clamps are loosened by vibration during use. The fuel tank is normally a separate entity, and is also lashed on deck during passage.

To start the outboard, follow these general procedures:

1. **Connect fuel tank hose to engine** and lock in place, if applicable.
2. **Pump hose grip** several times to build fuel pressure to engine.
3. Check to see that **engine is in neutral** and that dinghy is secured to yacht.
4. **Turn choke on.**
5. **Turn throttle to "start" position.**
6. **Pull starter cord** until engine fires.
7. **Push in choke** as soon as engine runs smoothly.

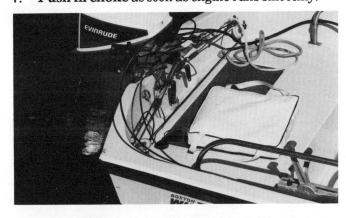

Figure 5-20 *Outboard motors are usually put on and taken off the dinghy many times. Special care should be taken to adequately secure the motor.*

Sometimes the engine will fail to start and the carburetor floods. If this happens:

1. **Close choke.**
2. **Shut throttle.**
3. **Pull starter cord** several times until engine fires.
4. **Put throttle at "start" position.**
5. **Pull starter cord again.** Engine should start.

Be sure the engine is well warmed up before engaging gear.

To stop the engine:

1. **Reduce throttle to idle.**
2. **Engage neutral.**
3. **Press Stop button.**

If you have finished running for the day, disengage the fuel tank before stopping the engine and allow it to run until all fuel in the carburetor is used up.

Figure 5-21

Handling the Outboard Dinghy

Handling an outboard dinghy is simplicity itself provided you obey some basic rules:

• **Never overload** the boat.
• **Trim the crew weight carefully**, with people at both ends of the dinghy and the heaviest weight amidships. If you are running alone, sit as far forward as you can, and go at a speed consistent with the nose up trim.

• Always **increase speed gradually** and never reduce it suddenly, never making excessive turns that raise the risk of tipping over the dinghy.
• Always **maintain a sharp look-out**, especially in anchorages or snorkeling areas where divers and swimmers may be operating.
• **Never allow people to trail their feet** over the edge, and check that the painters are coiled inboard.
• In shallow water, **use the outboard with caution** and tip it up in favor of oars when there is danger the propeller will ground.

Figure 5-22 *Weight distribution in the dinghy becomes critical when lots of people and gear load into the small boat.*

Coming Alongside and Beaching

The trickiest moments of dinghy handling come when you steer alongside a swimming ladder heavily laden, or beach ashore. Coming alongside:

- **Approach the yacht from astern** (or downwind) at a shallow angle. Reduce speed to a crawl.
- **Alert a crew member** to hold the ladder as you come alongside.
- About 10 yards out, **bring your dinghy parallel to the yacht** about 2 feet away at barely forward speed.
- **When drifting range is reached, put engine in neutral**. As momentum of boat slows, crew take hold of the ladder.

If you have approached at excessive speed, you can use reverse to slow you down. But excessive bursts of speed may result in the engine tipping out of the water.

Figure 5-24 *Correct timing of wave sets is vital to beaching a dinghy.*

Beaching

1. **Reduce speed offshore outside** the breaker line. Watch for the best spot to land, where sand is smooth and wave sets are smoothest.
2. Choose a smooth set and **motor in at moderate speed**, riding crest of wave or just behind it. Reduce speed but maintain steerage way.
3. **Stop engine just before waves break and tilt up engine**. Bow crew member jumps overboard and pulls boat ashore. Remaining crew assist. If not already done, engine operator tilts engine up on bracket.

In rough seas, it is better to use oars, tilting engine out of the way.

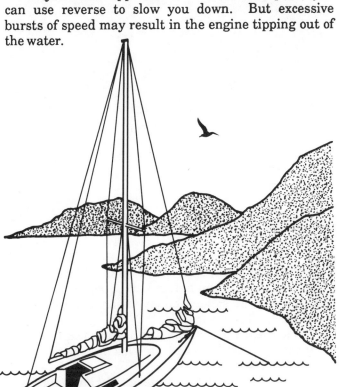

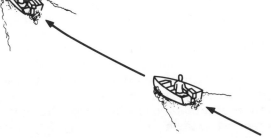

Figure 5-23 *Like any other boat, a dinghy should approach a yacht beam to beam.*

Launching

Except in very calm water, someone is almost certain to get wet when launching a small dinghy through breakers. This is no hardship in tropical waters, where charter dinghies are most commonly used on beaches.

- **Carry or drag the dinghy** down to the water's edge. Place the oars in their rowlocks.
- **Watch the breakers**. Identify a spot where the waves break smoothest, and look for the sets to identify cycles of higher breakers. Plan to launch immediately after one of these cycles has ended.
- As the last wave of such a cycle breaks, **run the dinghy out through the surf** with one or two crew members holding the boat head to sea. As soon as she floats, the oarsman gets in and starts paddling offshore.
- **The boat is held steady as long as possible**, then the other hands scramble in as she clears the breakers. WARNING: a fiberglass or other design of "hard" dinghy can tip over if boarded over her side rather than bow or stern.

Launching takes nice timing and practice makes perfect. However, even the most expert crews get wet sometimes.

Figure 5-25

Figure 5-26 *A spinnaker pole can offer sleepers great relief by keeping the dinghy away from banging on the hull.*

The Dinghy at Night

If you leave your dinghy on a towline aft at night, you may have an unwelcome visitor in the small hours — a bumping bow nudging at your stern. You can sleep well by using several alternative means of securing her:

- **Tie the dinghy alongside** against a cushion of fenders, secured fore and aft. This works well in smooth water.
- **Rig your spinnaker pole** at right angles to the mast with fore and aft guys. Secure the dinghy towline to the end and trail the boat astern well clear of the yacht. Better when there is a surge.
- A hoary old favorite that works well with galvanized buckets. **Lash a bucket full of water over the stern** of the dinghy. The weight of the filled bucket will keep the dink clear, theoretically at any rate.
- You can **haul the dinghy partially out of the water** and attach it to the anchor rode.

DEALING WITH UNEXPECTED SITUATIONS

The remaining AFLOAT SKILLS in this Section are those needed to cope with unexpected emergencies, situations that may never arise in the course of a lifetime of chartering. But it is well to be prepared for them.

Running Aground

You are certain to run aground several times in your sailing career, especially if you charter in tidal waters. You can run aground under all kinds of circumstances, like, for example:

- When you misjudge the depth when entering an unfamiliar port or anchorage. Perhaps you misread the chart.
- When you miscalculate the depth at low tide in an anchorage.
- When chart datum differs from actual conditions.
- As a result of dragging anchor and drifting ashore.
- When forced out of a deep water channel by heavy traffic.

Take comfort! In most cases you can get off in a few minutes. It is rare that going aground is a serious emergency.

If you run aground under sail, your subsequent actions depend on the wind direction.

The most likely circumstances under which you will run aground when tacking is at the edge of a narrow channel. With luck, only the deepest part of your keel will ground.

1. **Immediately tack**, leaving the jib aback.
2. The boat should swing round. **Keep the jib backed** until you are fully on the other tack.
3. **Bring jib over** and sail off the ground.

Sometimes, using your engine to help the turn is advisable.

Figure 5-27a *A backing jib (above) can help heel the yacht and get it off the ground. Quick reactions are usually the key to this method's effectiveness.*

If you run aground when running or reaching, the wind will be blowing you onto the ground, which makes it imperative to reduce sail.

1. **Try jibing,** in the hope you can sail off a shallow patch. Most commonly, this is impracticable.
2. **Lower sail.** Ensure all sheets are safely inboard, so they do not tangle round the propeller.
3. **Start engine and try reversing off.**
4. If this does not work, **lay out an anchor,** and use both engine and anchor winch to move the boat into deeper water.

Should you not be able to move the boat within a short time, whatever the point of sail:

1. **Load the bow or stern anchor** (whichever is most likely to be most useful) into the sternsheets of the dinghy.
2. **Row the anchor out into deeper water,** at an angle where hauling on it will either turn the yacht or tow her clear. Lay out as much line as possible.
3. Once the anchor is down, **the crew haul in on the line** on the anchor or sheet winch, combining the pulling momentum of the anchor with the engine to haul clear.

If the anchor is well snubbed, this can be a very effective way of getting off.

Some of these methods may seem very laborious if you are used to just shifting your weight or rocking the boat to get off the bottom, as is often done on grounded 20 ft. to 30 ft. vessels. However, such simple techniques do not normally work on larger vessels, so you have to rely more heavily on your anchors.

Dragging ashore while anchored probably means that you will ground but lightly. In these circumstances, start the engine and try motoring off while hauling on the anchor. If necessary, re-lay the anchor in deeper water using the dinghy, just as if you were laying a stern anchor.

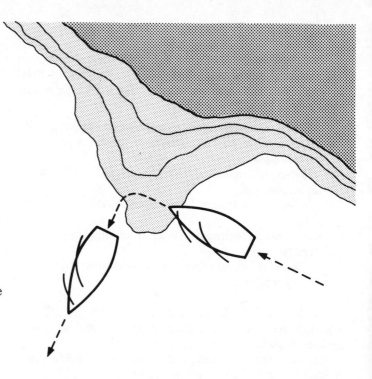

Figure 5-27b *When boat grounds while reaching or running a quick jibe may free the vessel.*

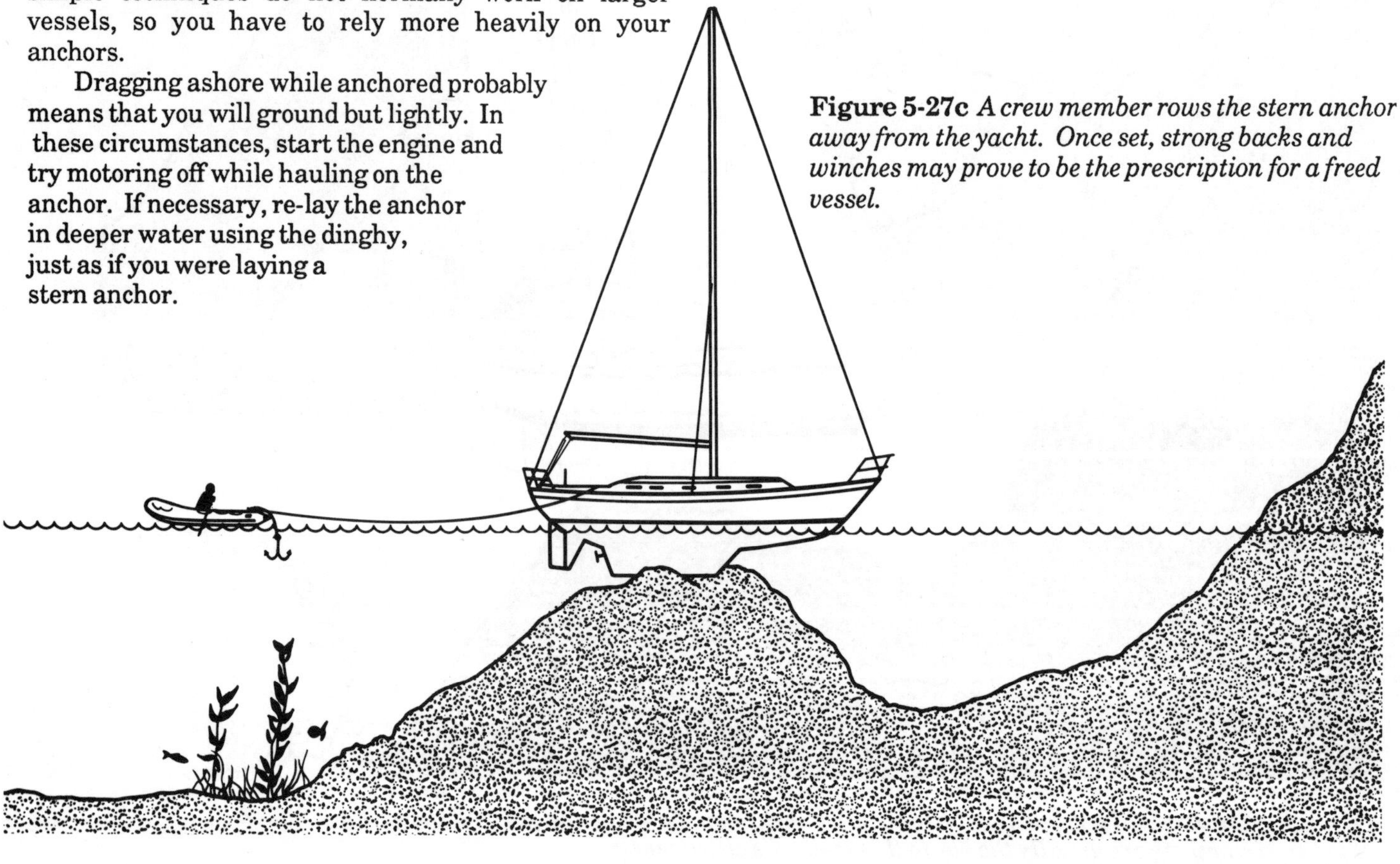

Figure 5-27c *A crew member rows the stern anchor away from the yacht. Once set, strong backs and winches may prove to be the prescription for a freed vessel.*

Three fundamental points however you ground:

• If there is a danger you will drift further aground, lay an anchor into deep water AT ONCE.

• Always **check that there are no lines overboard** to foul your propeller. This is especially important when anchored bow and stern and one or both of the anchors drag.

• **Beware of overheating the engine**, especially in sandy water, as the sand can block the water intake.

Going aground in tidal waters is no problem if you ground on a rising tide. You simply lay out an anchor, or turn the vessel toward deeper water, and come off with the rising tide, even if this means a wait of an hour or more. Remember that the greatest rise and fall is in the middle two hours of the tide.

Grounding on a falling tide is far more serious, for you are working with less and less water. Follow the procedures above, but work fast in case you are grounded until the tide rises again six hours later.

If you are stranded, you will have to wait it out. Since your vessel is a deep keel yacht, she will heel over as the water falls, perhaps as much as 45 degrees if the ground dries out completely. You should take some precautions:

• **Lay out an anchor** in the direction of deep water, so that the yacht will not drift further ashore when the tide refloats her. You can also use it to pull your boat out to deeper water.

• Use the crew's weight or anchors and other heavy objects as well as the boom to **ensure that the yacht grounds with her keel toward deeper water**. This will prevent water washing into the cockpit when the tide rides and before she comes upright.

• If the ground is rocky, try padding the hull where it will touch bottom.

• **Stow sails** and coil all lines carefully clear of the propeller.

• **Prepare food** for the crew while the vessel is till upright.

When the water rises, you can then haul yourself off without trouble.

• If possible, **send all nonessential hands ashore.**

The most dangerous tidal grounding situations arise only rarely, when you accidentally ground at the top of the spring tide, when the water reaches heights it may not reach again for weeks, even months. Exercise extreme care during springs.

All these grounding situations assume normal weather conditions and non-emergency situations. In extreme emergencies, you may have to be towed off, or even abandon the vessel. Your charter company will give you instructions about such (highly unusual) situations. You should, of course, contact them by radio if such an emergency arises.

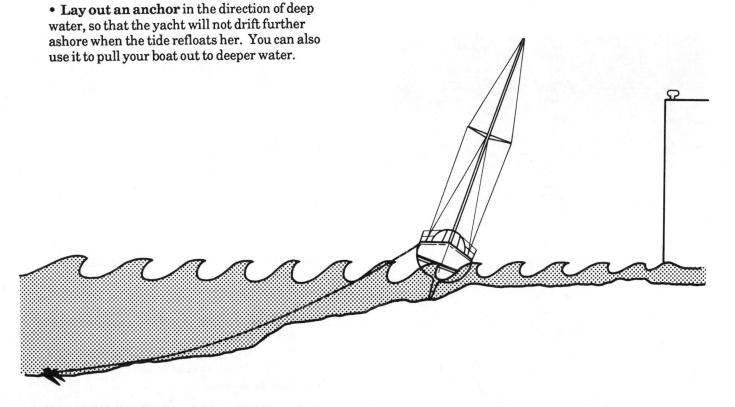

Figure 5-28 *In an area with a falling tide and swells, an anchor set in deeper water will keep the yacht from being driven further ashore.*

Lines Around the Propeller

Lines entangle themselves around propellers at the most awkward moments. A careless crew member allows a loop of jib sheet to trail in the water, you catch on a mooring line, or a dinghy warp wraps the propeller shaft as you go astern without warning. Fishing nets, plastic bags, and other debris can entangle your propeller, too. Clearly you must clear the obstruction at once.

1. **Try reversing the propeller** *slowly*, while the crew maintain tension on the offending line. You can sometimes unwind the line.
2. **Stop the boat** and send someone over in the dinghy with a boat hook. You can sometimes disentangle the jam from the surface.
3. If this does not work, sail into shallow, smooth water and anchor. Then send a swimmer over with snorkel goggles and a knife to cut the obstruction clear, or to unwind it.

If you are in open water, try to avoid sending down a swimmer in rough conditions. If you have to, attach a safety line to the strongest swimmer aboard, and work out signals to be used to haul him or her up suddenly.

TURN OFF THE ENGINE WHEN CLEARING propeller OBSTRUCTIONS.

Figure 5-29 *Helmsman slowly reverses the engine while crew members help retrieve a fouled sheet from the propeller.*

Figure 5-30 *Emergency tiller in use.*

Wheel Steering Malfunctions

You are sailing happily along and the wheel suddenly turns in your hand. The yacht sails in circles, or comes into the wind. You look below and find that a wheel steering cable has snapped.

1. If under sail, **try heaving-to or balancing the boat** on a set course if possible. Use engine if necessary.
2. **Start engine** for emergency maneuvering, but leave it in neutral, idling, unless needed.
3. If in shallow or confined waters, **anchor clear of traffic.**
4. **Locate emergency tiller** in cockpit locker and ship it as demonstrated by charter company.
5. **Resume passage**.

A wise skipper checks the wheel steering cables regularly for fraying and keeps them well lubricated and adjusted.

Springing a Major Leak

You are sailing along five miles from land, enjoying a smooth passage, when someone goes below and reports water rising over the cabin sole. You have sprung a major leak of unknown cause.

1. **Turn on bilge pump. Slow down vessel** by throttling back or reducing sail.

2. **Check bilges for obvious source of leak.** The most likely causes of a major leak short of hitting an underwater obstruction are:
   - broken hose on a sea cock, especially engine intake.
   - broken sea cock, or fractured hose clamp.
   - bilge pump outlet not hooked up, causing sporadic leaking when vessel heels.
   - problem with propeller stuffing box (this is unlikely to lead to a major leak).

3. If cause is obvious, **try and stop water flow.** Some possible remedies:
   a. If hose is broken, turn off sea cock valve. If possible, replace defective hose or clip from spares aboard.
   b. If sea cock proves defective, hammer piece of wood into orifice, or even rags and paper towels. Cover plug with plastic bag and lash tight.
   c. If hose has fallen off, close sea cock, reattach hose and tighten clip. Open valve and test.

4. If you are unable to check water flow, **man emergency bilge pump,** as well as starting main pump. If necessary, organize a bucket chain to keep water clear of engine and battery.

5. Head vessel into shallow water, call charter company on VHF and await instructions.
   Above all, do not panic. Few leaks are so catastrophic as to require immediate abandonment of your ship.

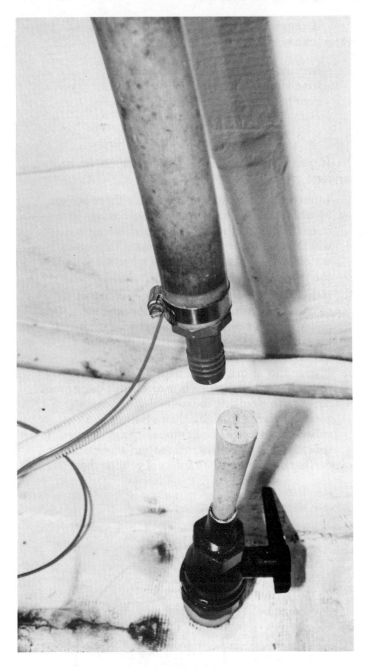

Figure 5-31 *Wooden plugs are the best temporary cure for a faulty sea cock.*

Dragging Anchor

Dragging anchor is usually due to these four major causes:

- An inadequate snub into the bottom.
- Inadequate scope laid out.
- Poor holding ground like weed.
- Someone else fouling your anchor.

If you drag anchor and there is no immediate danger:

1. Immediately **let out more scope** if there is room astern to do so. This will check most dragging in moderate weather. Re-snub to determine whether holding ground is adequate. Maintain watch to see that the additional scope is holding the vessel.

2. If this does not work, or anchorage is congested, **start engine and hoist anchor**, reanchoring in a new spot. This time double-check your snub and lay out adequate scope, as well as, verifying holding ground.

3. If your anchor drags because it is fouled by someone else, **recover your anchor,** taking great care to avoid cutting the rodes if the anchors remain entwined. **Reanchor clear of the offending vessel.** Under these circumstances, it is better that you move rather than experience further doubt about the safety of your anchor.

If you drag and there is immediate danger of grounding or obstructing neighbors:

1. **Start engine** and use motor to take strain off the anchor rode, while you assess situation.
2. **Recover anchor** and **anchor in a safer place**.
3. **Maintain anchor watch** to be sure you are not dragging again.

This completes Section 5 of the chartering course, and you are ready to take the certification test.

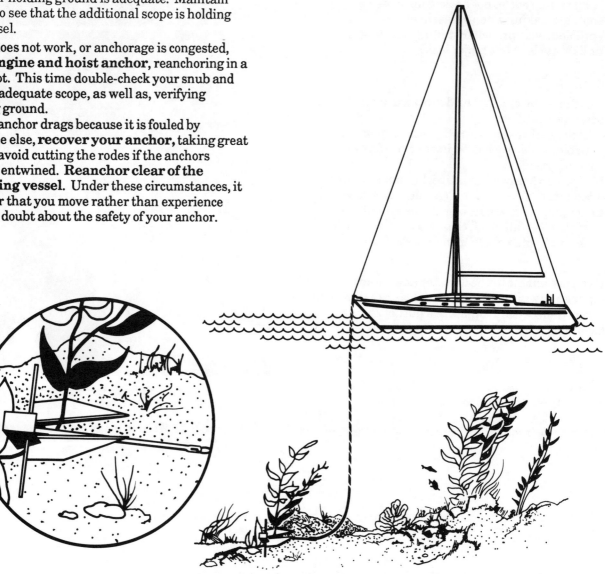

Figure 5-32 *Inset shows an anchor which is not buried sufficiently in the bottom to hold the yacht. An inadequate snub, inadequate scope, poor holding ground and fouling by another anchor could all contribute to the problem.*

EPILOGUE

Congratulations! You have successfully navigated from the front cover to the back cover of Chartering Fundamentals. Perhaps this manual was given to you by an instructor as a vital part of an intermediate sailing course. Maybe a bit of the curiosity which centuries ago drew sailors to the sea guided your hand to this book on a shelf. Either way, you have chosen to further investigate and clarify the art and science of sailing. For this, you should be commended.

The knowledge gained by reading Chartering Fundamentals solves only part of the developing sailor's puzzle. The remaining lessons lie where our navigating forefathers' satisfied their curiosity, upon the water itself.

In sailing, practice makes perfect. Each lesson in Chartering Fundamentals offers Ashore Knowledge (theory) and Afloat Skills (practice). Readers who have enjoyed this book outside an organized course should be aware that reading is a great way to begin learning. But only in the doing, the time spent underway, will your true education become complete.

Review this book regularly as you practice your skills. There will always be something new to learn, or something that you did not fully understand the first time around. Expert sailors are people who react instinctively to situations. They anticipate, prepare, and make cautious, considered decisions at sea.

Next

Once you have mastered the Ashore and Afloat portions of Chartering Fundamentals, make sure you are tested by an AMERICAN SAILING ASSOCIATION Certified Instructor at an affiliated sailing school and have your ASA Logbook signed.

What after that? Your options are infinite. You can sign up for the Coastal Navigation Course, a home study course or winter classroom program that will keep you active in sailing while shorebound. This course teaches the skills needed to become a highly competent basic navigator, capable of navigating successfully in the most advanced of bareboating areas, where tides run strong and the weather changes hourly.

Fortunately, there are many ways to ease into the world of bareboating. A growing number of charter companies will accept the AMERICAN SAILING ASSOCIATION Bareboat Chartering Certification as sufficient qualification for you to skipper on your own. Many developing sailors may find that the area, the equipment or the complexity of the skipper's responsibilities dictate some cruising under supervision. **A wise sailor knows his or her limits!**

Cruising and Learning

Many charter companies, especially in Florida and the Virgin Islands, run special week-long cruises that are designed specifically to build the beginning skipper's confidence. These are often run in the off season, when fleet yachts are less heavily booked and professional skippers have time to spare. This makes the courses an attractively priced way to learn more about bareboating. Contact the company of your choice and ask about "cruise and learn" packages.

The World of Bareboating

You can charter a yacht in almost any cruising area of the world these days. So you can match your skill to the demands of sailing waters in every climate imaginable, from New Zealand to Sweden, Greece to the Caribbean. The problem is to choose where to start and how to prepare for a charter in these exotic places.

At this point, we recommend you acquire Brian Fagan's definitive book on chartering, Bareboating (published by International Marine Publishing Company, Camden, Maine in 1985) not only builds on on the basic skills you learned in Chartering Fundamentals, but is a mine of information on the major charter areas of the world. It is a course on its own and deals, among other things, with the following questions:

• What are the best charter areas for beginners and more advanced sailors?
• What skills do I need for each area?
• What are ideal charter yachts? What gear should they carry?
• How do I decide on an area, a company, a yacht?
• What should we take with us. How do we make travel and yacht reservations?
• What about provisioning in different areas of the world?
• How do I prepare for a cruise in strange waters? What resources are available for this?

This book is almost an advanced course on its own. It is particularly useful in reinforcing and elaborating on basic skills, and for its hard-hitting advice on planning charter itineraries in such places as the Virgin Islands, Tahiti's Leeward Islands, and the Aegean. If there is a charter skipper's bible, this is it!

So tuck Chartering Fundamentals under your arm, gather some adventurous crew, rub on some sun screen and head for the harbors of the world. Remember that knowledge breeds safety and safety assures enjoyment and enjoyment is what the world of bareboat chartering is all about.

Good luck in the world of chartering!

Bareboat Chartering Standard Checklist

This checklist for the Bareboat Chartering Standard can be used as a guide for what you have or are about to learn. It also itemizes the minimum skills an individual should possess, in addition to those outlined in the ASA Basic Coastal Cruising Standard, before taking a 30-50 foot cruising sailboat on the water.

CHECK OUTS

- ☐ Engine Daily Check
- ☐ Engine Weekly Check
- ☐ First Aid Kit
- ☐ Tool Kit
- ☐ Stove
- ☐ Electronics
- ☐ Hull
- ☐ Rigging
- ☐ Sails

SAILING EFFICIENCY

- ☐ All points of Sail
- ☐ Tacking
- ☐ Jibing
- ☐ Sailing to Weather

MANEUVERING UNDER POWER

- ☐ Docking
- ☐ Turning (Confined Space)
- ☐ Stop Within 4' of Marker
- ☐ Bow-To or Stern-To Docking with Anchor

COLLISION REGULATIONS

- ☐ As Opportunities Arise

VHF

- ☐ Sending and Receiving Calls

OPERATING THE STOVE

- ☐ Proper Safety Checks
- ☐ Proper Lighting Techniques
- ☐ Proper Extinguishing Techniques

TOWING DINGHY

- ☐ Safety and Efficiency Techniques

SOUNDINGS

- ☐ Electronic and Manual Depth Checks

SAIL COMPASS COURSE

- ☐ To and From Destinations

MAN OVERBOARD

- ☐ Two Return Methods, Two Recovery Methods

NAVIGATION

- ☐ Lay Course Line
- ☐ Determine ETA
- ☐ Identify Landmarks
- ☐ Fix Using Bearings
- ☐ Depth Using Chart

PILOT INTO UNFAMILIAR HARBOR

- ☐ Use Chart and Natural Surroundings

ROPE WORK

- ☐ Rolling Hitch
- ☐ Trucker's Hitch (Cinch Knot)
- ☐ Bowline

ANCHORING

- ☐ One Anchor
- ☐ Two Anchors
- ☐ Bow and Stern

INDEX

INDEX

APPENDIX

A --- Answers to Review Questions

B --- Glossary

C --- Basic Check Lists

D --- Bibliography

E --- ASA Membership Application

APPENDIX - A   ANSWERS TO REVIEW QUESTIONS

SECTION 1

Question 1
   B, A, C, E, D

Question 2
   D,B,A,C,E

Question 3
   a. PFDs.
   b. Throwable PFD.
   c. Fire Extinguishers.
   d. Visual Distress Signaling

Question 4
   a. Anchor Windlass
   b. Furling Drum
   c. Bow Cleat
   d. Furling Line

SECTION 2

Question 1
   a. Foul weather gear.
   b. Boat Shoes.
   c. Knife and Spike.
   d. Changes of clothing.

Question 2
   a. With a bight of rope and the main halyard.
   b. With the aid of the dinghy.

Question 3
   C.

Question 4
   a. The stern.
   b. Starboard Spreader.

Question 5
   B.

Question 6
   A.

Question 7
   B.

SECTION 3

Question 1
   a. Oil level.
   b. Alternator belts.
   c. Water level in heat exchanger.
   d. Fuel level in tank.

Question 2
   a. Electrical tape.
   b. Sail repair kit.
   c. Alternator belts.
   d. Engine hoses.
   e. Water pump impeller.
   f. Spare lamp globes.

Question 3
   C.

Question 4
   Having completed repairs or filled fuel tank, loosen nut on injector supply pipe, choosing the one closest to the main injector pump. Then pump the manual lever on the injector pump until all air bubbles are pushed out of the tube and fuel flows freely. Tighten nut and start engine normally.

SECTION 4

Question 1
   a. All electrical, manual, electronic systems in order.
   b. Sails and running gear rigged ready to set, including reefing lines.
   c. Ground tackle properly secured, ready for use.
   d. All emergency gear aboard and in working order, crew able to locate same and use it.
   e. Bilges pumped out.

Question 2
   True

Question 3
   A.

Question 4
   9 feet

Question 5
   B.

Question 1

Check to see that sea cocks are open. Turn on water intake at head, then pump soil down pipe with pumping lever, using steady, firm strokes. After about a dozen strokes, turn off water intake valve. Continue to pump to expel all waste from outlet pipe. Clean bowl with brush or toilet paper, using water pumped into the bowl, then pump dry. Finally, close sea cocks.

Question 2
a. By smothering fire with a blanket.
b. By pouring water on the flames.

Question 3
C.

Question 4

Turn on gas supply at the bottle, then switch on stove switch at main electrical panel, if one fitted. Then switch on Gas Solenoid Switch. Finally, operate the stove as you would a domestic appliance.

Question 5
C.

APPENDIX - B GLOSSARY

Advection fog. Fog that forms when warm, moist air blows over a colder surface and is cooled below its dew point.

Anchor bearing. A bearing from a yacht at anchor to a landmark ashore; taken to check that the vessel is not dragging anchor.

Bahamian Moor. Lying at anchor with two anchors set at 180 deg. to one another.

Bareboating. Cruising under sail or power; where a sailor charters (rents) a yacht from a charter company or individual and assumes responsibility for skippering the boat him or herself.

Binnacle Cover. Compass cover.

Boom Gallows. A permanent rack designed to carry the weight of the boom when not in use.

Boom vang. Main boom control that leads from the boom to the foot of the mast, designed to control mainsail shape.

Cabin sole. Cabin floor.

Chart datum. A baseline used on charts which coincides with lowest, low water.

Cocked Hat. A small triangle of ocean between three position lines when you plot a fix on the chart.

COLREGS. International Regulations for the Prevention of Collision at Sea.

Compass Head. Compass heading of the vessel.

Crewed Chartering. Cruising under sail or power; where a sailor charters a yacht complete with professional skipper and crew and assumes no responsibility for skippering the vessel.

Cunningham. A line at the gooseneck designed to control tension of mainsail luff.

Dead-Reckoning Position (DR). The position of the vessel calculated on the basis of compass course steered, yacht speed, and allowances for tide and current. A position established without fixing the ship with landmarks, radio beacons, or other means.

ETA. Estimated Time of Arrival.

Harbor Stow. Stowing and securing the vessel at anchor or in harbor after a passage is over.

Hand-bearing Compass. Portable compass used for fixing the ship's position.

Heaving-to. Bringing the yacht to a complete stop under sail.

In Irons. A yacht is in irons when stuck in the eye of the wind, unable to pay off on either tack.

Land Breeze. A breeze that carries warm air heated over the land offshore at night (opposite of sea breeze).

Lee-bowing. Using tide or current flowing against the lee bow to push the yacht to windward.

Lubberline. A fixed, vertical wire in the compass bowl that is aligned with the yacht's bow.

PFD. Personal Flotation Device (Life jacket).

Pre-heating. Using a glow-plug to heat the injectors of a diesel engine when cold.

Position Line. A line-of-sight from your (unknown) position to an identifiable landmark.

Radiation Fog. Fog that forms over low-lying land on calm nights, creating a temperature inversion when the land cools the air immediately above the surface.

Rafting. Securing two or more yachts together at anchor.

Scope. When anchoring, the amount of anchor line over the bow.

Sea Breeze. A wind caused by hot air from the land rising, allowing cool sea air to flow underneath it toward the land.

Sea Cock. A valve that lets water in and out of the hull for specific purposes.

Self-tending boom. A boom set on a swivel on the foredeck, usually for a jib or staysail.

Ship's Head. Same as Compass Head.

Standard Port. Major ports where tidal data are recorded.

Sternway. Steerage way astern.

Tidal Range. Difference in the height of the tide between extreme high and extreme low water. The daily range is the difference for a specific day.

Topping Lift. A rope used to take the weight off the main boom when the sail is stowed.

Traffic Separation Zones. Shipping traffic lanes that are used in congested waters to separate shipping moving in opposite directions.

Wing-and-Wing. Winging out the jib on the opposite side to the main.

APPENDIX - C
BASIC CHECK LISTS

Preparing for Leaving the Slip

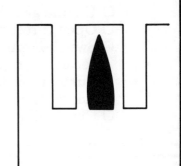

- ☐ Open hatches and ventilate yacht. Check for propane or holding tank fumes.
- ☐ Turn on engine compartment blower.
- ☐ Turn battery switch to BOTH.
- ☐ Check bilges and pump out.
- ☐ Ensure there is a PFD aboard for each crew member.
- ☐ Stow all loose gear.
- ☐ Close and secure hatches and opening ports.
- ☐ Explain trip to crew and delegate tasks for casting off.
- ☐ Turn on electronics and VHF radio.

Preparing for a Coastal Passage

- ☐ Check that all mechanical, electrical, and electronic systems are in proper running order.
- ☐ Rig sails, running gear, and reefing lines ready to set.
- ☐ Ground tackle properly secured and ready for instant use.
- ☐ All emergency gear aboard, in working order, and crew instructed in location and use.
- ☐ Fuel, water, and cooking fuel tanks full.
- ☐ All provisions aboard, stowed for sea.
- ☐ Navigational equipment in order, charts and pilot books for cruising area aboard.
- ☐ Head and stove functioning properly, crew instructed in their use.
- ☐ Bilges pumped out.
- ☐ All personal baggage stowed away for sea.

Follow the checklist for leaving harbor in addition to this list.

Preparing to Cast off

- ☐ Station crew on dock to handle lines and fenders.
- ☐ Look over side for trailing lines.
- ☐ Disconnect shore power cable and stow away.
- ☐ Unlock steering wheel brake and check rudder centered.
- ☐ Make final check of engine gauges.

Starting the Engine

☐ Run engine compartment ventilators.
☐ Check fuel gauge and battery condition.
☐ Check engine decompression lever pushed in and fuel on.
☐ Engine gear lever in neutral.
☐ Open throttle control to starting position.
☐ Switch ignition to preheat position and wait 15 to 20 seconds for glow plugs to warm up.
☐ Turn key or press starter button.
☐ Adjust throttle to comfortable warm-up speed.
☐ Check all gauges for correct engine operation.

Stopping the Engine

☐ Close throttle to idle.
☐ Put gear lever in neutral.
☐ Pull out decompression lever.
☐ When engine stops, turn off ignition switch.

Harbor Stow

This checklist is used when you arrive in port, but are not necessarily leaving the vessel.

☐ Check cleating and lead of anchor line(s). Install chafing pads if necessary.
  Stow mainsail on boom, secure with ties and cover.
☐ Unhank jib and stow in bag if necessary. Coil and stow sheets.
☐ Coil all loose lines and stow away.
☐ Rig awning or Bimini cover if necessary.

Secure Ship

☐ Stop engine, turn off ignition.
☐ Turn off engine switches at electrical panel (if any).
☐ Battery switch off.
☐ Check that automatic bilge pump is engaged.
☐ Turn off electronics.
☐ Centralize wheel and engage wheel brake.
☐ Connect shore power cable, if any.
☐ Check fenders and lines, also tighten halyards.
☐ Close hatches, take off personal gear, lock up.

ENGINE MAINTENANCE CHECKLISTS

Daily Checklist

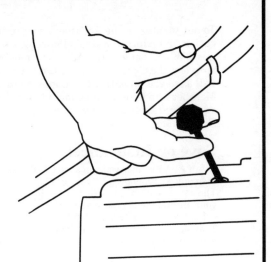

- ☐ Engine oil level.
- ☐ Alternator belts correctly tensioned.
- ☐ Fuel level.
- ☐ Water level in heat exchanger.
- ☐ Engine sea cocks are open.
- ☐ Now warm up the engine, then check:
- ☐ Oil pressure within acceptable range.
- ☐ Batteries are charging properly.
- ☐ Engine temperature is within acceptable range.
- ☐ Water coming out of exhaust outlet.
- ☐ Gear and throttle controls functioning properly.

Weekly Checklist

- ☐ Battery water levels at correct level.
- ☐ Transmission fluid level.
- ☐ Engine water intake is clean.
- ☐ Fuel filter bowls are clean.

APPENDIX - D BIBLIOGRAPHY

Chapman, C.F. Piloting, Seamanship, and Small Boat Handling. 57th ed. Hearst Publications, New York, 1987.

Fagan, Brian M. Bareboating. International Marine Publishing Co., Camden, Maine, 1984.

Fagan, Brian M. Anchoring. International Marine Publishing Company, Camden, Maine, 1985.

MacLeod, Rob. Sailing Fundamentals. American Sailing Association, Marina del Rey, CA, 1984.

Pyzel, Mike. Coastal Navigation. American Sailing Association. Marina del Rey, CA, 1987

Rousmaniere, John. The Annapolis Book of Seamanship. Simon & Shuster, New York, 1983.

Sleightholme, J.D. This is Basic Sailboat Cruising. Sail Books, Boston, 1977.

Sleightholme, J.D. Better Boat Handling. Seven Seas Press, Newport R.I., 1983.

Taylor, Roger. The Elements of Seamanship. International Marine Publishing Company, Camden, Maine, 1985.